ALLIED DUNBAR
RETIREMENT PLANNING GUIDE

ALLIED DUNBAR
RETIREMENT PLANNING GUIDE

by

Barry Bean
Tony Foreman
and
Dr H Beric Wright

Longman Professional

© Allied Dunbar Financial Services Ltd 1985

ISBN 0-85120-976-9

Published by

Longman Professional and Business Communications Division
Longman Group Limited
21–27 Lamb's Conduit Street, London WC1N 3NJ

Associated Offices

Australia   Longman Professional Publishing (Pty) Limited
130 Phillip Street, Sydney, NSW 2000

Hong Kong   Longman Group (Far East) Limited
Cornwall House, 18th Floor, Taikoo Trading Estate,
Tong Chong Street, Quarry Bay

Malaysia   Longman Malaysia Sdn Bhd
Wisma Damansara/Tingkat 2, 5 Jalan Semantan,
Peti Surat 63, Kuala Lumpur 01–02

Singapore   Longman Singapore Publishers (Pte) Ltd
25 First Lok Yang Road, Singapore 2262

USA   Longman Group (USA) Inc
500 North Dearborn Street, Chicago, Illinois 60610

Printed in Great Britain by Biddles Ltd, Guildford, Surrey.

General introduction

A dictionary definition of retirement is not particularly encouraging. It talks of people who have retired as having 'withdrawn from society or observation'. It means to go away or to retreat. It confirms that to retire often means 'to leave office or employment' and then adds, somewhat darkly, 'especially because of age'.

A better approach is to regard this time of life as a time of independence. We can all be independent of the need to turn up for work regardless of whether we want to or not — but we have to accept that we have no automatic income and no automatic salary increases. We can't change our independence and choose one with better prospects and perks — the independence we achieve will only be as good as the plans we have made for it.

Many people still tend to regard this part of their life as one of 'cutting back'. They tend not to see any prospect of improvement in the quality of their life. For many executives and even for people running their own businesses, retirement, or the thought of giving up work at all, comes as a shock.

The shock is largely due to the lack of preparation. Despite the considerable and growing publicity that has been given in recent years to the need to prepare for retirement, most people still don't. They still tend to regard retirement as a time of loss and although they may not fully appreciate it, what they actually need is some careful and considered help.

Organised support for people approaching retirement has developed only gradually in this country over the last thirty years. Now, however, with an increasing tendency towards taking early retirement, there is considerably more interest being shown in the need to help people prepare themselves for what could be a twenty or twenty-five year part of their lives.

There is a climate of greater understanding emerging and more importance is being placed on careful preparation for retirement. It is estimated that approximately 10,000 people each week join the ranks of the nearly 10 million who have already retired. Retired people currently account for approximately seventeen per cent of the total population — this figure could be nearly twenty-five per cent of the population by the end of the century.

For most people, the basic ingredients of a happy and successful retirement are a stable environment of home, friends and interests, satisfactory health, adequate financial circumstances and a sound personal philosophy of life. Most are agreed, however, that for the majority of people approaching retirement, finance is the main concern.

The major challenge is to go on thinking positively and constructively about life. This can often be a particular problem for executives. Work offers more than just a means of earning money — it offers status and a sense of identity and for them, the loss of employment can be very similar to bereavement. The trauma may be even worse if retirement comes earlier than expected.

Beric Wright, who has contributed the section on health and philosophy to this book, is no stranger to the executive world. He is able to draw on a wealth of experience in helping to prepare people for the 'evil day' (because that is how they look upon it), helping them to shake themselves free from the dependency on full-time employment. Having something to do, planning their time, keeping active and healthy, recognising their new found independence for what it is, are all part and parcel of helping to look at retirement as positively as possible. One of Beric Wright's constantly recurring themes is the need for couples to plan this new-found independence together. He is all too familiar with the picture of the busy executive completely immersed in his job, with bulging briefcase a regular feature of the evening and weekend conversation — or lack of it. He is aware of the re-adjustment that is necessary when husband and wife are living closely together for perhaps the first time in their lives — facing a future of 'Sunday lunch seven days a week' can often put a considerable strain on the best of relationships.

His recommendations are strongly based on reality. The statistics are relatively straightforward — men tend to marry women younger than themselves and women tend to live longer than men. The majority of planning (and certainly the majority of *financial* planning) should take into account the very high probability (but not certainty) of the wife being left on her own resources for the last years of her life. However, it is so often not done this way.

As far as financial planning is concerned, these facts cannot be ignored if the plans are to have any chance of fulfilling their basic objective — which is to maintain a reasonable standard of living for as long as you live. Clearly, it is impossible to estimate accurately the duration of retirement, but it is also rare to make use of the information that helps to assess the probabilities. The common advice is the simple statement that the life expectancy of the average man of sixty is about eighteen years.

This is an interesting statistic in itself but not particularly helpful as far as financial planning is concerned.

Of far more use to the people planning for retirement are the life tables which are used by life assurance companies to calculate their premium rates. These show, not just the life expectancy of a man at any age, but the chances of him living a further ten years, or fifteen years, twenty years, or whatever. If you tell a man aged sixty that his life expectancy is eighteen years he may form an immediate mental 'picture' of his financial plans and the overall structure that they might take. If you tell him that he actually has an almost 50/50 chance of living beyond the age of eighty, he may start to think about his financial plans in a slightly different light.

A typical life table starts off with 100,000 individuals at birth and records how many of them die each year until, at age 100, there are virtually none left. It's a simple matter to adjust these tables so as to start off at age fifty-five or sixty and this has been done below.

The tables show how many out of 1,000 people of a particular age will live to a particular age. Because the table starts with 1,000 people in each case, it is able to show the chances of survival to any particular age. Thus, 805 out of every 1,000 men aged sixty will live to age seventy, whereas 654 will live to seventy-five and 475 to eighty. This clearly is much more useful than the simple information that the average sixty year old will live for eighteen years.

A useful feature of these tables is to follow Beric Wright's thinking and to look at the chances of survival for a husband and wife together, expessed in pure mortality terms, of course. This knowledge is absolutely vital for sensible planning.

Let's take the case of a husband aged sixty and a wife aged fifty-five — which represents a typical retirement age of a husband and a typical age difference between husband and wife. The table shows that:

- 654 out of every 1,000 men aged sixty will live to age seventy-five.
- 878 out of every 1,000 women of age fifty-five will live to age seventy.

It follows that (if we assume that they are all married) 87.8 per cent of the wives of the 654 surviving men will also be alive.

That means that 574 couples will survive or, put another way, there will be eighty widowers and 304 widows.

In nearly two thirds of the cases, either the husband or wife will have died after twenty years of retirement. The survivor may have another ten years to look forward to and this is often overlooked in financial planning. Most men almost take it for granted that 'the survivor' will be their wife. However, for those couples where only one life survives twenty years, one fifth of those survivors will be the male life.

In their chapters on financial planning, Tony Foreman and Barry Bean examine a wide range of issues from the choice of investment to the increasingly popular idea of retiring abroad. They lay a lot of stress on the need to keep plans flexible and to make sure that a careful distinction is drawn between immediate financial needs and longer term planning for income.

The key word of course is 'planning'. The road to hell may be paved with good intentions but it was never more true when planning for our own independence. There are so many things which need to be planned for: continuing an income, preserving the family home, avoiding unnecessary taxation and avoiding unnecessary family disputes and turmoil. Despite the real rewards of planning for the future most problems arise, not because people have made incorrect plans but because they have made no plans at all. Even the most successful of businessmen can damage his own independence by inactivity and neglect.

In the other books in the *Allied Dunbar* series (particularly the best selling *Tax Guide*) there is frequently a chapter or list of ideas on how to save tax, or how best to arrange your affairs. In the same spirit, but with a slight variation, here's a list of popular fallacies about planning for your future independence.

Planning for the future:

- is only for couples
- is only for the rich
- is only for the elderly
- is expensive
- is not for wives or members of the family
- is simply a matter of making a will
- is a once-in-lifetime job
- is only concerned with life assurance

We are all living longer. Medical care is better, we look after ourselves more with diet and exercise, modern surgery can help to refurbish some of the worn out bits — and we are retiring earlier.

It's time to start planning for it.

Males				Expectancy (Years)	Females Age				Expectancy (Years)
Age									
					55	1000			27.6
60	1000			18.6	60	977	1000		23.2
65	919	1000		15.1	65	939	961	1000	19.1
70	805	875	1000	11.9	70	878	899	935	15.3
75	654	712	813	9.2	75	784	802	835	11.8
80	475	516	590	6.9	80	648	663	690	8.9
85	290	315	360	5.0	85	472	483	502	6.4
90	136	148	169	3.6	90	279	285	297	4.4
95	44	48	54	2.5	95	118	121	126	3.0

Acknowledgements

The publishers acknowledge with thanks the assistance given by Professor D E James, David Hoppitt and James Wootten in preparing material for this book.

Contents

PART TWO: FINANCIAL ASPECTS

Part One
Health

1 Problems and priorities in retirement

Facing retirement

Not long ago at a small pre-retirement seminar for senior managers and their spouses, we had — with the aid of the ubiquitous flip chart — an enlightening discussion. Each of the participants was asked to suggest a problem or priority in their retirement thinking so far. One of the wives surprisingly came up with the vital need to have a plan for each day. 'To make it worth getting up for', her husband remarked.

This is in practice one of the critical decisions about retirement. Some fear it, others resent it and an increasing number look forward to the last day at work. I can speak personally from both the academic and the practical angles because after twenty years of struggle to make the Pre-Retirement Association (PRA) viable, I personally retired from full-time, largely managerial work, two years ago. I was fairly certain that I knew what to plan and had collected more than enough commitments to keep me involved. But having had a round of embarrassingly friendly social retirement events, I suddenly found that on the day after my sixty-fifth birthday, I had nothing to do. The diary was blank: there was no office to go to, nothing specific to be responsible for and no secretary to organise my day.

In spite of all my knowledge and homework, it was a shock and although I still had contacts and non-executive roles, I did feel lost for several months. It took this time to learn to restructure my life, adjust to new priorities of my own making and, I hope, become a more relaxed person. And of course I was lucky because I did have several different roles, some new things to take up and additional income from some of them. Interestingly, too, about three months later I suddenly realised that

I felt quite different — and very much better. I realised that I was no longer chronically tired. Busy people as they get older learn to function effectively against a background of considerable fatigue, not properly relieved by the holiday quota.

I can assure readers that being busy and involved, but not over-tired, is a major benefit of retirement. You suddenly realise, as I did, that over the last few years you were seldom at your best.

I do not want to boast or preach too hard and will, after this, stop reminiscing, but it struck me that a less well-prepared person who really was faced with blank weeks stretching ahead would probably feel bemused, sad and lost.

Part of my advice on contingency planning for retirement, and in my view quite the most important part, is to realise that work not only pays the rent and provides a standard of living but, more importantly, is responsible for one's status and identity. Without this a retired person is in danger of becoming a 'non-person'. As such he and his wife are in danger of drifting rudderless in a sea of trivial and meaningless pursuits. They may well lose their disciplines, and become indulgent lotus eaters surrounded by other 'non-people'.

A second critical benefit of work is that it provides association with other people. You may not like them much but at least they are there, even if only to rail against. It is a fact of life that people need people and appreciate being wanted. Loneliness we know is the main emotional problem of getting older, particularly if you live alone, or you are unmarried.

All of which is why the seminar wife talked such sense when she said 'we must have things planned to do'. There must be entries in the diary. As she and her husband had not yet retired, this showed a great deal of insight and understanding. They should have no major problems.

Over the years of talking, writing and advising about retirement, we have established that the main areas of decision are as follows, and they make quite a tidy branched logic or critical path picture. They are in strict order:

(1) What are you going to do, how do you propose to spend your days?
(2) Where will you be able, or want, to do these things?
(3) What sort of house will be best as your base, ie, should you move to a smaller house or even a bungalow?
(4) How much money will you have or need to live on and would it be sensible to earn more?
(5) What about your health and what should you know and do to optimise it? There is, in fact, a lot you can and should do.

To this very basic checklist, I think it is worth adding a further point which is the need to review relationships with one's spouse, the rest of the family and the social circle. Most wives look forward to seeing more of their husbands and having time together. But if communication has been poor and the relationship a bit negative, there may be a strain. Marriage may be for better or worse but not for most of us at the level of seven lunches a week. This implies a lot of role change and rethinking.

Clearly too, family needs and priorities will influence decisions under the first three headings and must be thought through. After the war when we started a family my mother, who was a busy doctor, announced firmly that she had brought up four children and was not going to do it again. She was an academic but rather inactive grandparent. Most of you will probably be looking forward to more involvement but there are pitfalls and you must beware of losing too much of your independence. However, family needs may play a large part in determining, for instance, where you want to live.

Finance and money management are the kernel of this book and require the best possible advice. I can say this with some experience because one knows that professional people, particularly doctors, tend to be bad at looking after their own affairs. And businessmen may be better at making — and possibly spending — money, than they are at managing it for their old age.

But I should like to end this section on a note of caution, perhaps prejudiced by my own attitudes and somewhat puritanical approach. Over the years I have been worried by the impression that a lot of people look forward to retirement as a continuous holiday. Enough money, no responsibilities, swimming and drinking in the sun and so on: all made easier by the financial benefits of the Costa Somewhere.

This may be fine for some but by retiring to Spain you are opting for a very negative life: pure pleasure, without involvement or responsibility becomes very boring and remote from the real world. A recent article by a friend of mine, who really ought to have known better, listed all the sybaritic virtues of Spain — golf, swimming, cards, drinks, sun, etc. But do you really want to be a useless person retreating into an unreal enclave of non-contributory life? If you do opt for a foreign residence it is both prudent and civil to take the trouble to learn about the country and to speak the language. To live permanently somewhere and not be able to communicate with the citizens is both arrogant and insulting.

My personal advice is remain in local circulation, go on contributing to society and only holiday on the Costas.

The demographic scene

Although the frail and lonely elderly have long been recognised as a group in the population requiring support and shelter, it is only over the last twenty-five years that the retired group has become recognised as presenting separate and different problems and needs. In about 1960 the National Corporation for the Care of Old People began to feel that the 'young elderly' needed specific thought and advice. They set up a broadly based exploratory group called the Pre-Retirement Advisory Committee.

This group, of which I was a member, established, at least to its own satisfaction, that this was a problem area requiring attention. Consequently we set up on our own as the Pre-Retirement Association and had a long hard struggle to establish an independent base and develop the requisite support.

What has happened in demographic terms is that many more people are living longer. Initially it was not so much that life expectancy was increasing, as that more and more people were living out their full term. This in itself was nearer four than three score years and ten. Since then life expectancy is beginning to increase so that we now have a situation in which large numbers of people remain active until well after eighty and those in sheltered housing are often in their nineties.

Taking the population as a whole and adding in the move towards earlier retirement and, sadly, redundancy, we have a situation in which roughly a third of the population are retired and living on pensions. The parallel growth of occupational pensions has also to a degree increased the incomes of this group.

When, for instance, we started the retirement magazine *Choice*, we were told that it was doomed because there would be no advertising revenue as the target readers had no disposable income and were all on the breadline. This proved, as we suspected it would, to be nonsense and after a spluttering start the magazine has proved to be a useful success and now has competitors but no serious rivals.

It has succeeded because it provides specific advice (for those about to retire, or who have recently retired) on finance, housing, health and activities. What has been constantly encouraging is the accounts by retired people of all the fascinating and exciting things they have managed to do: some of them for purely constructive and contributory pleasure, others as second, or even third careers, to supplement their incomes.

What has happened is that better housing, higher standards of nutrition and health care have reduced the toll of deaths in childhood and middle age. Thus more people retire in fair health and, given sensible management of their lives, can now expect to live twenty or more years in retirement. But much more important is the realisation that these 'young elderly' people may well have ten to fifteen years of vigorous potential. They are in no way frail or feeble and are capable of considerable activity and contribution.

It is critical that you, as an about-to-be or recently retired individual, realise this. You are *not* going on the shelf to waste away: you may well deteriorate if you don't try. Given, however, the will and the determination, you can go on much as before. Brain and muscle power can be preserved and developed, but this must be done as a conscious policy and you must not allow yourself to drift without targets.

This same population trend is true of all the developed countries which are increasingly working towards the provision of better recognition of, and facilities for, the retired. In America, for instance, they have raised the retirement age but I doubt if this is the right way round the course. The pace of administrative, business and productive life is now such that most kitchens get too hot for the sixty year olds. In any case, the route to the top must be kept open for younger people.

What is still required in this country are better facilities for part-time work, the total abolition of the earnings rule and a better advisory network about involvement at a variety of levels. It would clearly be politically dangerous and socially undesirable for a third of the population to become separated, isolated and aggrieved. Equally it is sensible that they should remain more or less evenly distributed across the country and not collected into retirement enclaves.

Obviously some parts of the country and indeed other countries, like Spain, have a better climate and a more pleasant environment but it is unwise in my view to encourage the development of large concentrations of retired people, as in Florida and, to a degree, our own south coast. If integration and involvement in the local community are the keys, groups of inward-looking older people must be dangerous for themselves and the local community.

I have watched the drift to Spain and similar places with alarm. It may be fine to spend a year or five lazing in the sun and getting better value for your money but before taking this decision it is wise to think ahead to ten or fifteen years hence. What will it be like to be a foreigner growing old in another country, surrounded by a diminishing group of ageing expatriates dreaming of home and the good old days and increasingly losing touch with home and family? In this connection the problems of illness and frailty have also to be faced. Adequate medical care and resources must be available wherever you are. These problems are discussed in Chapter 5.

There is another demographic problem that bears on this, which is the fact that, for reasons we don't understand, women live appreciably longer than men. This means that part of your contingency planning for late retirement must include thought not only about possible frailty but also about what will happen when there is only one of you. Life in Spain, for instance, for an elderly widow must be a fearful thought, compared with being near the family or in a granny flat or Abbeyfield house, close to friends.

Because of this longevity and greater potential for activity, it has recently become apparent that we need to rephrase our advice about retirement planning. It is now clear that it is probably sensible to think about and plan for two distinct phases of retirement.

The first is obviously the phase of activity and involvement with very little diminution of faculties but more opportunities for doing the things that you both want to do, at a reduced pace and not under time pressure. In this respect I can assure you that once over the readjustment, busy though you may be, it is liberating to know that you don't have to do anything you don't like or feel behoven about. Everything you take on is your own choice and can be dropped tomorrow if it does not suit or becomes frustrating. For this phase, it may not be necessary to make much adjustment in lifestyle or living. You will probably find that your money goes further than you thought it would. The mortgage may be paid off, school fees finished, National Insurance and pension contributions stopped and so on. Income may drop but so does tax, so that on balance you are less worse off than you feared. I know that there are financial advantages in having a mortgage but psychologically there is a lot to be said for being and feeling free and this may help your spouse. If you want to earn a bit and were previously salaried, there are tax advantages in being self-employed.

Having decided, as previously outlined, what you are going to do and where, the next vital point is housing. If you decide to stay put, your present house may well do for the time being or longer. But if it is too big, has or has not a garden and so on, there may be a case for a smaller or more appropriate house in more or less the same area.

If you decide to move, for family or other reasons, the pros and cons of which are discussed later, it is worth giving a lot of thought to the sort of house that will carry you into phase two, ie, given a choice there is a case for thinking ahead and remembering that there may come a time when stairs are difficult, you may not be able to drive and ultimately there will only be one of you. In essence, however, little change may be needed and I am strongly in favour of staying where your social roots are.

Phase two, the period of frailty and diminished mobility, may require change. As I have said, if change is decided on earlier, the phases may be merged but if not, more special accommodation will have to be provided and a possible move nearer better medical facilities or to a sheltered housing unit. I do know of one family who are now in their third generation of granny flat occupation, with the younger generation taking over the main house and their parents in comfortable independence round the side. All this may sound gloomy but I can assure you that it is best thought about in good time.

The real message in these first two sections is that as you are likely to be about for another twenty years, it is far too long a time to drift about doing nothing in particular. Retirement does provide opportunities and challenges to restructure your lives and it is the meeting of new challenges that keeps you young and lively. Grasping this nettle requires thought and effort but it is well worth it. An increasing number of eighty year olds remain in active circulation and I do hope that you will opt for this alternative.

Doing little and living in the emotional past is not the best recipe for survival.

Attitudes and activities

The other day I met a friend who had been retired about a year and he looked very well, cheerful and lively. After telling me about all the things that he and his wife were doing, he finished up by saying that looking back a little he was wondering how he ever had time to work. This seemed to me to be an ideal state in retirement. As you will read in the more detailed health section, health is very much a function of well-being and if morale and satisfaction are high, there is no time to be ill or diseased.

There are all sorts of facets to early retirement but the most important thing is to accept it, at the lowest level of resentment as a necessity. At the highest level, it should, if not positively welcomed, be regarded as an opportunity to re-plan life and priorities and do new things.

The person who drifts into retirement with a feeling of resentment, will be miserable, no fun to be with and is very likely to become depressed and diseased. These are the people who don't draw their pensions for long — they fade away.

In the Pre-Retirement Association we preach that retirement planning should start about five years before the day. This may be a bit idealistic but the experts do say that the best financial planning does have this lead time (see Chapter 6): But as an alleged expert in the behavioural aspects of retirement I would advocate serious thought and discussion being given to the problems, and plans laid to deal with them, at least two years ahead. A few companies facilitate this by building in a diminishing working week over the last year or six months. In this way the job has been taken over and you are used to filling the non-working days: and your spouse will be getting used to having you around.

There are several good reasons for this advice. The first and probably most important is that it gently conditions you to the thought, starts you on the planning trail, begins to generate things to look forward to and minimises the chances of becoming bored and resentful.

Second is that if you decide to move to a new area, which may be a risky business and is discussed later, you can get this organised and begin to grow new social roots and get to know people and possibilities. If you already have a second home which you propose to make your new base, this is a much lesser problem. The nicest thing that happened to us when we gave up London, was an invitation to a drink next door which turned out to be a friendly event to welcome us full time to the village. As we had considered selling the house because it was

rather large, it was particularly encouraging to be welcomed —
we had made the right decision.

The third reason is the possibility of beginning to learn new
skills and develop a wider range of interests and activities. As I
have said, activities and involvements are critical and they
don't just happen; they have to be planned. We do have in this
country, although it is creaking a bit under government auster-
ity, a fine adult education network which is there to be used.

I aim this advice particularly at the workaholic and the professional person with few outside interests apart from those
which are work-related. Not only are you likely to be a rather
boring person, you will find it more difficult to maintain morale
and establish a new identity. It is also worth noting that old
dogs can learn new tricks — and skills — but only if they are
prepared to try.

To reiterate the crux of my message, you must be prepared for
retirement and have a discipline of physical and mental stimulation. So, against this background, what are you going to do
and what will be in your diary? The possibilities are legion and
you have to decide your priorities.

How to spend your time

For both of you, assuming that you are married, these choices
are critical and should, I suggest, be made fairly flexible
because as the situation evolves your views may change with
experience. It seems sensible initially to take on slightly too
much over the first year. This helps the transition from work to
retirement and can provide a range of choice after about a
year, ie, you can weed out one or two commitments that turn
out to be boring, too demanding or involve a lot of travel. It is
also important to realise that if what you want to do is professional or work-related, it is wise to get it organised at an
early stage. Several people I know have been surprised by how
quickly they were forgotten. It seems easier to remain in circulation than to get back into it again. Some years ago I met a
man who had gone off on a nine month world tour and
returned to find many of his possible slots filled.

It is wise at this stage to make a rough decision as to how much
time you want to spend together, do things jointly, and the

extent to which your activities should be separate. It is probably unwise, for instance, for both of you to be on the same committee!

At a recent seminar, the point was made that it was easy to step into the position of being an exploited grandparent: the children taking the view that now you are retired you can be considered a convenient dumping ground. Your schedules can easily be disorganised by too much baby-sitting and you may find that large doses of young grandchildren are exhausting. It may be helpful in this respect not to have too many spare bedrooms.

Obviously this decision rests largely with the wife but she should remember my mother's view and on the whole lead her own life. Clearly if there is a health crisis or marriage break-up priorities may be altered.

Professional people, such as doctors, accountants, lawyers and senior managers, do have the advantage that because of their qualifications and experience they can go on working either at a reduced rate or in a consultancy or non-executive role. It is, however, surprisingly difficult to switch from the executive to non-executive role in your old firm and I suspect that for both parties it should not continue for more than a very few years.

It is also important that the temptation to continue exactly as before should be resisted. It is much more stimulating to do new things, work on a different network and perhaps acquire new skills and interests.

Another factor in settling these priorities is to have a clear idea as to how far and how often you are prepared to travel and be away from home. In my view this should be minimised because travel, and driving in particular, becomes more demanding as you get older.

Gainful or voluntary activity

You will already have done a rough budget for your retirement and should thus know whether or not it is essential for you to supplement your pension and savings on a regular basis. This decision clearly determines your priorities, what you look for and possibly where you live.

I would suggest that the younger you are the more you are likely to need income and indeed the more sensible it is to have the disciplines of an earnings-related commitment; part-time work can be rewarding. If the need for income is marginal, you can opt for a range of voluntary or caring activities which may well pay expenses, and be pleased when the odd fee or gainful chore comes along.

Wives and single people will have to make similar decisions and it may well be easier for women to find part-time paid work. But the decisions having been taken, the next step is to look around for contacts to get you suitably involved and enrol in training or educational courses.

Gainful activity

It is obviously not sensible to try to list all the various ways in which it might be possible to find a part- or full-time job which uses your experience and meets your inclinations, but several points are worth making.

First, probably the easiest way, at least in theory, is to start a new enterprise or offer a service. This requires imagination, guts and a bit of capital, but with your experience you ought to know how to run a business and control stock and cashflow. The pages of *Choice* magazine over the years are full of successful second careers, usually at the service level.

Secondly, there are a number of organisations which exist to help older people find jobs at various levels and some of these are listed at the end of this chapter.

Thirdly, it is wise to accept that any job you take on is likely to be at a lower level than you were used to and, indeed, you probably want less responsibility, particularly for staff. It has often worried me that business and managerial people sadly made redundant tend to look for, and usually fail to find, jobs at their previous level. One needs to be prepared to start again and justify one's skills rather than be taken at a possibly tarnished face value. In all sections of our community there is still a huge need for services and to get things done reliably at a reasonable rate. If I needed to do this, for example, I would start a jobbing gardening facility and trundle my spade and mower round, tidying up and fixing the garden for the frail and disinclined. There is a crying need for this, certainly on the fringes of the larger cities and even in the country.

Fourthly, there is the vital need for association with other people to replace one's 'old work mates' and this is where service activities are both important and useful. Even working part-time in a shop provides lots of contacts, if also a few frustrations.

Our world is full of things which need to be done and there are plenty of people about able and willing to pay for these. It may sound menial but could be exciting and rewarding. One of my dreams, and we nearly did it once some years ago, is to start a community based activities centre or facility exchange. People who wanted to do things would bring in their skills and others wanting a service would buy it or contribute something different. One or two units like this do exist and flourish. Why not consider starting one on your patch?

I make no apology for the fact that what I have outlined here is both obvious and to a degree platitudinous but what I have tried to do is very simply to set out some alternatives to start you thinking.

Voluntary work

Here again the scope is endless. Our society is largely based on self-help as distinct from Local Authority welfare. There is a host of organisations providing this assistance from, say, the National Trust to Meals on Wheels and Day Centres. They need both workers and administrators and organisers. Many also need fund raisers but this is a difficult task which does not often appeal.

It may sound a bit pious but I do think that it is reasonable to urge competent and previously busy people to seriously consider ploughing something back into the community. This can be both necessary and very rewarding because we all need to be wanted and to have others relying on us. Your contacts and contributions may even help your own old age.

There are lots of local and national bodies crying out for participation and my own favourite example is the Abbeyfield Society. This consists of a countrywide network of autonomous local societies working on a common formula, providing homes for the lonely elderly. Each society is financially and administratively independent. It acquires houses which are converted into six or more bedsits with a housekeeper, and provides a home for those requiring care and company. As the need is growing, Abbeyfield requires all the organisational help and support it can get, particularly from the recently retired. This is to start new societies and to take over from older members to give committees new blood. One must remember that this type of voluntary work is just as valuable to the participants as it is to those who benefit directly from the charitable service provided.

There cannot be any community or part of the country where there is not some need for more help and in most areas there are organisations, like the local Council of Voluntary Services, Citizens Advice Bureaux, Town Hall, public library and so on which will tell you about what is available.

As with my suggestions about activities centres, there is a need for setting up groups of retired people to support each other, discuss problems and do things — both active and social. Such a group, once established, could put pressure on the locality to provide more facilities for the retired, from part-time jobs or educational courses, to special physical activity sessions in keep-fit and swimming.

Amusing yourself

As well as the types of involvement outlined so far, you need to plan time to do a number of your own things. All the 'things' you have always wanted to do but never had time for. They can be active or passive, indoors or out and, preferably, both mental and physical.

It is sensible to leave enough time to enjoy yourself and develop new skills and hobbies. These will become more important as you get less active and less inclined to charge about on committees and to travel around. It is also important to build in time each day for some physical activity which will help to keep you fit and supple.

The trick, I am sure, is to hold a balance between the personal or domestic activities and wider involvement, and to have enough time for both. But I do think that it is dangerous to plan only for recreation: more of it certainly, but not full-time. I don't really believe that golf is enough of a full-time activity for intelligent people. And this is really why I worry about the concept of joining a retirement enclave in a warm country. Life may be pleasant, money may go a bit further, but it is barren and non-contributory, which must become boring and inward-looking.

More about moving house

If you look up bereavement in the dictionary it gives the meaning as 'to be deprived of'. I have already made the point that, unless properly handled and understood, work bereavement can bring the same consequences as perhaps the death of a spouse, depression, loneliness, guilt and resentment, etc. If at the same time you move to a new area because it seems a nicer place to live, you run the risk of double bereavement because you are a newcomer to a strange land.

The cottage down the lane, so lovely in the summer, may be less attractive ten years later in the winter, when you can no longer drive a car and have to carry home the shopping, or when there is only one of you living alone.

A couple of years ago we had a detailed and poignant case study from a couple who moved north two years after retirement to be near their daughter. Although they had thought through the problems and knew what they were facing, it took them two traumatic and lonely years to begin to grow roots in the new area and several times they nearly came back.

Retirement is a time when you need all the social contacts you have, to establish your new identity and activities. Thus by moving, the dice are loaded against you and it is difficult, particularly for older women, to establish a new social network. For this range of reasons our overall advice from the Pre-Retirement Association is to very careful about moving and to be strongly biased in favour of staying where you have mostly been. Of course there may be good reasons, like not wanting to be too much in a town, being nearer the family, a more clement part of the country, cheaper living, and so on, for moving but as a generalisation it is usually wiser to stay put, in perhaps a smaller or more appropriate house in the same locality.

With people being so much more fit and active into their seventies no change may be needed for some years but if you do decide to change it is wise to think ahead to potential frailty. Thus a bungalow, smaller house, flat with a good lift, etc, may be sensible. It also provides an opportunity to reconsider activities like gardening. Now is the chance to have a larger or smaller garden depending on preference.

A last point about moving is that if you want to do this there is a great deal to be said for trying to start the change a year or more before retirement by establishing a second home well in advance. An increasing number of people do so by having a weekend home out of town, with perhaps a much smaller work-related residence in town which is easy to give up. Again, particularly in terms of retirement, it is often easier to find modest part-time work in a small community. I have always been worried about too much commuting for older busy people which is an argument in favour of two homes if you can afford it.

Having said this, however, one does find that living in two places produces problems and we were always carting food, clothes, animals, etc, in and out of town. It was a great relief when this stopped and, as I have said, we did have contacts and activities in the village.

The value of your house or houses is another critical factor. For many people the lump sum of your pension and the paid-for house are your main assets and must be considered as part of the financial planning. It may well be wise, particularly later on, to consider capitalising the property to improve your financial comfort. In these days most of our children are doing at least as well as, and often better than we did at their age. They would rather have less worry about us than be left a large house to be sold. There is much advice about this topic in Part Two of this book.

At the time of writing we, in BUPA Hospitals, are selecting residents for a new pilot project in sheltered housing for the frail elderly who cannot cope on their own. One of the things we have to do is to make a financial assessment. In pursuit of this an old lady recently seen was reluctant to sell her quite large house because she wanted to leave something for her nephew. The nephew when contacted, with her permission, as he was the executor, was quite clear that he and his wife would be far happier to have their old aunt contented and comfortable, than hold out for the money. It is worth noting too that this conflict could have been mitigated several years earlier by more open discussion.

I have laboured the points about where to live because they are critical in retirement planning. They clearly relate to priorities about activities and being near the family and tend to be taken without properly thinking through their implications. It is also prudent to consider the time base involved and know whether you are planning for the rest of your lives, or a shorter period, followed later by somewhere simpler and more supportive. In this respect, it is wise to make the changes a little too soon rather than cope with, or even contemplate, the change involved at the onset of frailty or in response to a crisis.

Relationships, roles and anxieties

Retirement can impose a severe strain on the relationship between husband and wife. If you stop to think about it, married couples do not, on the whole, see all that much of each other. Weekends and holidays provide some opportunity for communication and joint activities but in relation to the rest of the year this is a small proportion of the time. If in addition the husband does a lot of travelling, brings work home and is out three or four evenings a week, the situation becomes more difficult.

I suspect that the overall situation has improved in the last decade but suddenly being thrown together can produce a strain on a neutral and not very strong relationship, particularly as the type of man involved is likely to be a workaholic with a wife who has allowed him to get away with relative non-participation for so long.

This is why I have laid so much emphasis on planning activities and establishing — or re-establishing — relationships within the family. The lack of these may be a reason why a few men, and possibly working women too, fear retirement and go on hoping that it will not happen to them. There is, therefore, subject to the need to remain in circulation, a case to be made for the equivalent of a second honeymoon.

As a culture we are not particularly good at adult relationships, with each other, with our own parents and with the children. Mothers tend to fret about the way in which their young conduct their lives and bring up the grandchildren. Many of them make this worse by continuing to see their children as still obedient and grateful but not adults living their own lives. The relationship, therefore, becomes more of a duty than a pleasure.

There is a genuine conflict here because the young are brought up, educated and pushed out into the world to be independent. This is fine and far better than having them exploiting their parents, not marrying, living at home and getting their shirts washed: the modern equivalent of the younger unmarried daughter who devoted her life to her mother and ended up in middle age as a lost soul without the experience of a real life of her own.

Equally, however, in social terms the family unit, and now the extended family, is critical for social stability. And a supportive family network is the best way to keep the frail elderly out of the clutches of the social workers and the Welfare State. To achieve at least some of this, the relationships have to be based on mutual respect and appreciation and not just a sense of duty.

The problems involved are, of course, long-term and dependent to a degree on the attitudes handed on to the next generation — but they do need to be worked on. In the section on health and well-being I have argued the case for more open relationships and a willingness to discuss problems, grievances and differences in a non-threatening and non-confrontational way. Our national non-emotional approach and the stiff upper lip militate against this openness. 'Carry on as before and pretend it is not there', may work when there is plenty to do but in retirement there may not be enough glue left to make the relationship stick.

I have already made the point that a decision has to be taken about how active you want to become as grandparents and there is no doubt that the generation gap makes for easy and joyful relationships between the older and the younger, provided of course that it does not produce conflicts with the parents in the middle.

What I am really urging at this point is that thought should be given to discussing differences before they become grievances and establishing some ground rules for minimising anxiety and developing a constructive social network to which all contribute. Without such a contribution you are unlikely to be wanted or appreciated and without it you are likely to be lonely, which is the biggest single problem of growing old gracefully. All this is why I am on the whole against a retirement pattern based almost entirely on recreation: be this the golf course in this country or the patio abroad. Real people in everyday situations provide a better stimulus and challenge than being a non-contributory drone.

What will happen when one of us gets ill and dies is inevitably something we all think about — or should do as we get older. This again requires discussion. It is, however, worrying to find the number of quite senior people who have not made or updated their wills: equally the number of wives, who are the most likely survivors, who may not know (1) where the will is, (2) who the solicitor is, (3) the executors and, most important, (4) how they are to pay next month's bills and what there will be to live on.

I think it is irresponsible not to discuss this situation and there is a case for the will, or some of it, to be the matter of a family council so that everyone knows where they stand. Bereavement is tragic and difficult enough, especially for the less resilient elderly. It can be made much easier to cope with if there is a plan to bring into action. If there is no such plan and nowhere set to go, it is wise to struggle on and avoid taking vital decisions until some of the emotional dust has settled and things are seen more clearly.

With grown-up children, houses are an under-used asset, empty soon after breakfast, tidied up an hour later and waiting for the evening. With the husband in and out all day the functional nature of the house changes, which changes and their implications, the wife must tolerate and even encourage. Soon after we opened our first Pre-Retirement Association offices in Clapham, a nice man walked in and asked if he could help in any way. His offer was taken up and he soon became an appreciated member of our new family. It transpired that, recently retired and on a small pension, he was turned out of the house by his wife after breakfast and told not to come back until lunchtime. All he could afford to do was to wander about or sit and gaze. Rather like the retired workman who watches his old mates go into work and then counts the bricks on the wall opposite his window.

Extreme cases these may be but at different levels they do illustrate a lack of understanding of the domestic changes in retirement. A well-organised non-working woman will have found a range of outside activities as the children grow up: indeed if she does little but housework she is likely to be bored, boring and vulnerable — but this is another story. But the last thing the wife should do is to give up her activities to look after her retired husband. What ought to happen is that, metaphorically, he should go on a cooking course, sweep the stairs and learn to iron shirts.

In this approach there is a generation gap. Our children are now sharing more of the domestic chores, doing the shopping and even some cooking from time to time; and very competently too. Retirement does give a chance, and includes a need, to re-think domestic roles and priorities and incorporate a greater degree of sharing than our generation was used to. This in itself is a new challenge and stimulus.

Not many men now expect to have their domestic lives served up without contribution but a few still do and their wives to a degree think that they justify their existence by being the waitress. I suspect, however, that the relationship will be better with more joint activity and such changes will be facilitated by some insight into what is required.

There will be more leisure and more time together. The main point I have been trying to make is that with the loss of work, relationships become more precious and do need nourishing. Like the whole of retirement planning, the changes are unlikely 'just to happen' but have to be contrived. With a third of the population retired, we have to demonstrate that we can and want to remain active and contributory members of society and that our experience and wisdom are useful and not threatening.

Useful addresses

Association of Researchers into Voluntary Action and Community Involvement (ARVAC)
Stephen Hatch (Chairman)
26 Queens Road
Wivenhoe
Essex CO7 9DL

Action Resource Centre
Henrietta House
9 Henrietta Place
London W1M 9AG

Age Concern
Bernard Sunley House
60 Pitcairn Road
Mitcham
Surrey

Employment Fellowship
T H Oakman OBE JP (Director)
Drayton House
Gordon Street
London WC1 0BE

The London Voluntary Service Council
68 Charlton Street
London NW1

National Council for the Single Woman and her Dependants
Miss Heather McKenzie (Director)
29 Chilworth Mews
London W2 3RG

National Council for Voluntary Organisations
Nicholas Hinton (Director)
26 Bedford Square
London WC1B 3HU

REACH (Retired Executive Action — Clearing House)
Victoria House
Southampton Row
London WC1B 4DH

2 Mental outlook and relationships

The framework

A vital point about successful retirement has already been made: namely that the cornerstone is continued mental and physical stimulation. One fallacy is that the older person inevitably faces a state of gradual mental decay. This is largely nonsense and it is easy to name men and women who go on being successful, creative and active well into their eighties — many even have the motivation to be successful in new fields of endeavour.

Another lie is that old dogs cannot learn new tricks. It has recently been shown, by research carried out at the Max Planck Institute in West Berlin, that 'pensioners' can be taught and have the capacity to acquire new skills and knowledge. Methods of teaching need to be different to provide the right stimulation, and sufficient motivation has to be there because it can be quite hard work but it is nonetheless perfectly possible. Retirement must be accepted as a period of about twenty years which provides the opportunity, and more importantly the challenge, to lead a new and different life. It is a chance to do new things, at a more gradual and less competitive pace, that should provide the stimulus to develop a new role and accept a second but useful and rewarding identity. And of course an individual's past skills and reputation can be exploited. Many people continue in much the same role and this keeps them interested and in circulation. But it is usually more exciting and therefore more stimulating to look for new challenges to broaden your horizons.

There are two further pieces of the stereotype which are more accurate but given insight can be overcome. The first concerns the ability to accept new ideas. It is commonly believed that all great advances in inventive thought are made by youngsters who have an intuitive flash and are prepared to follow it up. This is to a degree what Edward de Bono calls lateral thinking.

The problem is that as we get older we tend to become the slaves of our own experience and what is regarded as the perceived or traditional wisdom in a particular field. Also, of course, we have seen it all before and tend to be reluctant to face the hassle of change. This makes us reactionary and resistant to it. We are comfortable with what we know, understand and are used to. Any sort of change tends to be seen as threatening and to be resisted: all of which is reinforced by our own previous experience.

Thus, older people, unless they are careful to avoid the pitfalls, want to play safe and stay in the comfort of their rut. But this, if uncorrected, is a slippery slope towards minimal activity and is likely to produce decay. By understanding what will happen to your behavioural reactions, and fortified by the reassurance that abilities can be developed, successful retirement involves a willingness to accept the discipline of continued stimulation.

Having too little to do is the main danger to be avoided. Conscious choices have to be made to develop an appropriate retirement life style. The right things seldom just happen. The deprivation of work — a form of bereavement — has to be consciously replaced by new activity. It is the experience of most of us that long before retirement we tend to become more forgetful and fail to remember telephone numbers, shopping lists, etc. Older people worry about this and become afraid that it marks the onset of senility. It does not.

We now know more about how parts of the brain and nervous system function and consequently what causes, and to a degree, can cure, malfunction. The brain seems to be a cross between a computer and a switchboard. Like everything electronic, it gets less efficient as the insulation breaks down and the connections become worn. Also, like an ageing sound reproduction system, there is an increase in background noise or static which does not help efficiency. But on the whole the system goes on working, albeit more slowly. The way in which the memory works is not yet understood but there must be an indexed data bank in which information, or experience, is stored by imprinting. It must obviously be capable of access on demand by certain trigger mechanisms. It is common knowledge that most of us have good long-term memories. We can remember the past and our current reactions are formed by the interplay of personality and past experience. It also seems that as we get older our memory of early life tends to sharpen. But when it comes to remembering a telephone number, or all of three or four shopping items, memory fails in a rather unpredictable way. This is called short-term memory and is better in children than adults, perhaps because they do not have so much to remember and possibly because there is plenty of spare storage space. Clearly, too, this is a protective mechanism because the brain cannot go on remembering everything forever. Such a perfect filing system would have to be of infinite size. Thus short-term memory does fail with age for understandable functional reasons. Imprinting for retention has to be more positive, recall gets less efficient on marginal imprinting and the whole system is rusty because of wear and tear.

All this is normal and should give you no grounds for anxiety. I have found that my short-term memory is subject to fatigue. It is worse at the end of the day and when I am overtired. Part of the art of growing old gracefully and living in a family or other group, without becoming a drag, is to recognise, accept and discount these changes, thus minimising the impression of becoming a doddering old reactionary. Short-term memory is best dealt with by realising that it is prudent to write lists and memos — and then remembering to read them. Avoiding becoming the slave of your past experience or an institutionalised version of your younger self is much more difficult. Much of the change and many of the trends in today's life do not appeal to us older people. But, trite though it may sound, the world has always changed and it will be inherited and developed by the next generation. Strive for tolerance and understanding and be willing to turn off the personal gramophone record except perhaps for your wife, husband or good friends who either agree or regard it as an acceptable price paid for the rest of the relationship.

Another major change that happens with age is the increase in reaction time. This is the speed with which you can respond to changes or stimulae, like a hot kettle handle or a traffic light.

This is probably best seen in car driving, which requires skilled adaptation and response to a rapidly changing situation. Older people, particularly as they drive less, find it increasingly difficult to respond in time. Often the scene has changed, or the opportunity passed to overtake safely. The same is true for being a pedestrian or catching a bus. Again, there is nothing you can do about this but be brave enough, particularly in the case of driving, to stop in time to avoid an accident. I failed to stop both my parents from driving in time to avoid the predictable accidents which terminated their driving. Mercifully these only involved the write-off of two cars: both my parents were then over eighty.

There are two important morals here. The first is that learning can continue and that new challenges must be sought out and met. This is the key to remaining and appearing young and active. The second is that there are inevitable changes and limitations that come with age. They come at different rates and times but by understanding them and making the necessary behavioural corrections, their effects can be considerably mitigated.

I suspect, although it is impossible to prove, that the changes can be delayed by living actively and participating in life. Optimism and involvement are more rewarding than negativity and defeatism. Old dogs must be prepared to learn new tricks to go on surviving pleasurably.

Stress and relaxation

Stress is a popular, misused and badly understood term. Being stressed, or thinking that you are, has to some extent become a cult. Wives, for instance, like to describe their husbands as being stressed and harrassed. Similarly, the busy professional finds it difficult to admit that he is thoroughly relaxed and on top of the job. To be so is perhaps to have failed or be capable of doing more. In my terminology this is not stress.

We all need challenge to keep us going and provide stimulation. Challenge is, in fact, a biological necessity for all living things. Challenge, at various levels in our daily lives, successfully dealt with, is satisfying and exhilarating. It needs to come

PLANNING FOR INDEPENDENCE

Allied Dunbar has a range of plans and investments that are tailor-made for financial planning. If you would like further details (or if you would like to arrange a viewing of our video 'Happy Anniversary'), just return this card to us.

ALLIED DUNBAR

PRC 1

Name ....

Company ....

Address ....

....

....

Daytime Tel: ....

I would like to arrange a viewing of your video. ☐

Business reply service
License no:

Marketing Department
Allied Dunbar
P.O. Box 27
Station Road
Swindon SN1 1EL

from a variety of sources but only when the challenge becomes too much do we experience stress.

I think it is important to realise the difference between stress and challenge: the one being essential and desirable and the other being a potentially dangerous manifestation of overload.

The trouble is that the stress reaction, which is biologically defensive, as it were, to get you off the hook, happens at a sub-conscious level and we don't recognise the chain of cause and effect unless we have developed insight. The reactions too are many and various and I believe that they destroy well-being by causing illness, which is why I believe in the holistic approach to analysing the cause and proper treatment of symptoms.

An essential feature of this philosophy is to realise that we function at different levels on a range of networks. You may be good at some things and bad at others, the latter being stress-ful. All this too is very much a function of basic personality and past experience. Not all of us are good at people and relation-ships, and when in senior positions, or in the family, tend to be insensitive to the effect we have on others. We do not see our-selves as stressors, which is both unfair and unnecessarily painful to our associates. Tense, anxious and obsessive people, particularly if they are also introvert perfectionists, will obviously find life more difficult than relaxed extroverts. Although it is difficult to change personality traits, if they are understood it is easier to live with them, both for you and the people around you.

It must also be accepted that under-employment or lack of challenge is just as stressful as too much challenge. This is, of course, what may happen in retirement. The let down of no fixed routine and all the other losses of retirement can be stressful and produce the same sort of depression as is associ-ated with true bereavement, which is why it is essential to have plenty to do and people to relate to in a stimulating way. But if work as one gets older has become stressful, much of this should go with retirement which may then be seen as desirable relief. Tense, anxious people, however, may carry this on into retirement and find it difficult to enjoy their new lives.

Over the past few years there have been significant advances in developing and teaching relaxation techniques and what are called coping skills. These skills are particularly useful for tense executives and professionals of any age because they do help to reduce the strain of coping. They consist of a mixture of developing insight into the events which cause stress, and relaxation to deal with them.

I would recommend anyone, if they are a tense, highly strung worrier, to consider trying one of these techniques. There are several of them, including two sorts of yoga. They do produce tranquillity and also help sleep, and you should now have time to devote an hour or so a day to this. I know many older people who have found their lives much easier once they have learnt to relax and unwind.

There is plenty of literature about relaxation and I would recommend *The Alternative Health Guide* by Inglis and West, published by Michael Joseph. The essence is to find a method and teacher which suits you. Some adult education schedules now include relaxation classes which are well worth trying.

Sleep
Sleep is precious and if you are one of those lucky people who can drop off anywhere at any time, this section is not for you.

Mythology has it that older people sleep less well and dream more disturbingly than younger ones. There is no evidence for this but those who had sleep difficulties tend not to find it any easier, except of course when this is anxiety related and the anxiety is removed by retirement. I suspect that part of the mythology stems from two sources: lack of exercise and boredom. It is a truism but you do have to be tired in order to sleep or, put the other way round, it is hard to stay awake if you are physically tired. And doing nothing much all day, possibly eating too much as well, is not conducive to the relaxed tranquillity that going to sleep requires. A good flat bed with a hard mattress is desirable and the probability is that the bed you got married in, is not the one in which to die. If one partner sleeps less well or wriggles about, don't be too proud, separate beds may be a solution.

Warmth and comfort are obviously important to sleep and I have found that an electric over-blanket, preferably a double one with dual controls, is an admirable modern convenience for better sleep. In my view, too, the open window has no place for the elderly. There are usually only two cures for snoring: ear plugs or separate rooms. I believe that there is a place for sleeping pills although they are currently out of medical fashion: worth discussing with your doctor.

Much research has been done about sleep and sleep rhythms and it does not seem to matter much as to whether you get all your sleep at night or take some during the day. Individual sleep needs vary from five to eight hours and if it suits you, there is a case for a regular afternoon nap rather than getting all your sleep at night. Retirement is about doing what you want when you want. There is everything to be said for getting up at five, if you are awake then, and sleeping during the day. If you tend to drop off after supper and live with a younger family, a nap may make you less anti-social in the evenings.

You may also have found, in the few years before retirement, that you tire more easily and don't have the ability for sustained endeavour. This is a normal age effect and may be, to some extent, related to lack of exercise. As I got older I found that it took me much longer to recover if I became overtired. This again is due to age, anxiety and a degree of boredom with work. You have seen it all before. It is a good idea to be careful not to get overtired and irritable. Watch out for this and ask your spouse to and then take a break or get some extra sleep and relaxation. I suspect, too, that if you are actively involved there is a case for three or four breaks a year. They need not all be long ones. Fatigue is the enemy of enjoyment and well-being is the antidote to disease.

General tension and anxiety do make sleep difficult because although the muscles are still, the mind races and worries, usually in unproductive circles. Tense, perfectionist and obsessional people can't shrug these characteristics off in retirement. If you are like this, it may well be that here too a relaxation regime, of which there are now plenty about, will be helpful. They all depend on a trick or gimmick, which is fine. The problem is to find the one to suit you and offered by a convincing teacher with whom you have rapport. Early retirement is a good time to experiment in relaxation.

Relationships

When, twenty-five years ago at the Institute of Directors, I started to try to understand the health, rather than the disease problems of the members, I became inevitably involved in the emerging field of stress and what was then called psychosomatic medicine. This meant learning about the life style and pressures to which my patients were exposed. We soon realised that there were three main environments: work, home and leisure. This last is particularly important from middle age onwards and it is sensible to get pleasure and relaxation from totally different activities. In fact it is the antidote to workaholism from which so many of my patients suffered and which made them both vulnerable and boring people. They had no outside interests. It also became clear that nearly as much stress arose from domestic as from professional or work sources. The hard driving executive tended to neglect his wife and family, especially if he travelled a great deal. I found, too, and this was in the sixties, that these men often had difficulties with teenage children with whom they really had rather little contact. The problems then became stressful and produced feelings of guilt. As well as this we got the impression that many wives had a raw deal. They had had the income and the status but rather little real contact. To a degree this was their fault because they did not insist on a better and more human relationship. The situation has improved since then. Wives are both more demanding and, perhaps more important, increasingly involved in activity outside the home. One of my key questions to a man coming for a health check used to be 'what job satisfaction does your wife get out of being married to you?' Hopefully, if I got the timing right, this led to a rethink of the relationship — which is important in middle age, with the children growing up.

All of this highlights the importance of relationships. These become much more critical in retirement to fill the void created by loss of work and its associations. As a culture or society, I suspect that we are bad at relationships, which may be one of the factors responsible for the relative breakdown of the family and the consequent loneliness of the 'abandoned' elderly.

Some of this may be due to English reserve — the stiff upper lip and all that — plus an unwillingness and lack of tradition in discussing problems and difficulties openly and honestly. We also find it hard to treat our children as adults and rather expect them to continue in the childhood 'dependent . . . obedient . . . grateful' role. This makes them regard their parents as a duty and not a pleasure and may therefore limit contact with grandchildren. This is a pity because grandchildren can be precious in retirement and grandparents in their role can be very valuable to their children. But sadly grandmothers, particularly, can cause friction and tension by disapproving of the way in which the grandchildren are being brought up and trained. Some of this may be legitimate but much of it stems from the generation gap, grandparents tending to expect that the way in which children should be brought up is static, remaining the same as it was in their day.

A marriage that has rubbed along reasonably well at a rather superficial level, is often put under strain by much greater contact and perhaps an element of boredom. This can be made worse by a change of residence to a new area without an adequate social network. It is, perhaps, more difficult for a person whose life centres around the home to establish a new identity and they may become isolated and fractious.

This is not the forum to explore the problem in greater depth but I want to make the point and a plea for the need to rethink relationships. In some retirement seminars I have managed to develop useful discussions about relationships and to get couples to discuss, objectively and without acrimony, some of the quirks of their spouses that irritate them. If you are going to embark on the next twenty years of productive tranquillity, it could be sensible and useful, as it were, to have it out and start again. I think that there is a case for what might become a second honeymoon to start this off. There is also the problem of possible role change: the husband now has more time at home and need not be looked after so much. There is in fact every reason for encouraging him to look after himself and share the chores much more. It may be that a neutral counsellor, good friend or professional will help to get the dialogue going and keep the temperature down. There is nothing to be gained by starting a slanging match but much by becoming more open in discussing problems.

Another area requiring openness is the problem of planning what will happen when one of you dies, and usually it will be the man who goes first. Do you both know about wills, solicitors, executors and so on? Do you know how much money there will be and how immediately available it is? It is quite extraordinary, in otherwise seemingly responsible people, how little many wives know about what will happen to them when they are left on their own.

It is much easier to do all this before it becomes an acute problem and it is a legitimate area for family discussion, so that everyone will at least have a rough idea of a contingency plan. This will reduce some of the shock of bereavement and facilitate the inevitable readjustments. Death comes to all of us and it is sensible to know what we want to do about it.

The British are bad at bereavement, perhaps because it is badly handled by doctors and nurses, but also because our national reserve inhibits the expression of grief and friends are frightened to talk to us. Grieving is a natural and necessary process and unless it is encouraged, the process is halted and the survivors never re-emerge into reasonable social life. They remain bottled up with their memories and guilts. It is a good exercise and socially valuable to make a point of supporting any friend or relative who has been bereaved. If you talk to them afterwards, many will say that once the funeral was over nobody wanted to know them, largely because their friends were too embarrassed to talk through the situation.

The last area about which I have strong views is the question of discussing the possibility of death. If someone is dying of cancer, it is obvious to both the sufferer and the family. But how often do they all, encouraged by the doctors, pretend that recovery is still round the corner. Do make a point, now before it happens, that you want to know the truth about any illness and face up to it together and as a family. It may sound trite and patronising but I can claim that families who are quite open about what is likely to happen, at any age, and who share the whole experience are enriched by it. The sadness is easier to bear.

People do need people and we all need to be wanted. Relationships are most of what is left as we get older. In our society they seem to me to need better cultivation than they often get. This should not be too difficult for mature people.

Sex after sixty

It is difficult to write usefully in detail about sexual activity in older people. This is because of the wide, and completely normal, range of variation in both need and performance. But I think that it is fair to make the point that for most couples sex becomes less important in later life.

What is important, however, and this is probably the most important point in this section, is that couples should continue to express their affection in a physical way. Even if there is no complete intercourse, there can still be plenty of physical contact and conscious effort made to show that love and affection are fully maintained. It is a help if you do things for each other, show appreciation and don't take it all for granted.

Inherently there is no reason why sexual intercourse should stop until after seventy but folklore has it that it should. This is nonsense. The Victorian attitude that intercourse is something that should be confined to the reproductive phase is finally dying. Women should find the menopause liberating because the risk of pregnancy is no longer present and precautions do not have to be taken. In fact it can be a period of mild abandon. Any menopausal problems should be dealt with, if necessary by attending a special clinic. Today there is no excuse for tolerating severe symptoms for months or even years. It is hard on women that most doctors are men, many of whom remain in the 'grin and bear it' era of non-intervention.

A main problem for women is that there may be some dryness after the menopause but this is easily dealt with by a simple lubricant jelly or even a hormone cream. Here a doctor or clinic should help with advice.

Sexual performance and need in older people tends to be determined, firstly, by past performance and, secondly, by regularity. Those who may only have intercourse about once a month will tail off and find it more difficult than if it happens once a week or so. It will usually be found that stimulation and arousal take longer but this should make it more fun.

It is also sensible to stop the event falling into too set a pattern, as it tends to do without thought. New approaches should be tried and different times of day, or even different places, may help. Fatigue is the enemy of libido and as the run up to retirement is often a period of stress and fatigue, sex does tend to run down, leading to a feeling that this is the end of the sexual road. Again, this is not inevitable and a honeymoon atmosphere plus an increase in general well-being should reverse the trend. Difficulty tends to arise when the needs and abilities of you both begin to go in different directions and rather than doing anything about it, the situation is left to drift into one of no attempt and no success: plus a certain amount of guilt.

Men particularly may find it more of a problem to become aroused and then begin to feel guilty. Anxiety builds up and a vicious circle sets in. In spite of what the advertisements say, there are no magic remedies and on the whole drugs and potions fail to help in the long term. However there may be, a short-term placebo effect.

If the woman finds intercourse uncomfortable there is probably a physical reason and your doctor or a specialist should be consulted. The cause is nearly always simply dealt with. The main thing is to overcome any reluctance to seek advice. It is normal, reasonable and desirable to continue enjoying your sex life.

Should there be problems or difficulties, two steps can be taken. The most important is to be frank and open about them so that friendly discussion and understanding of each other's problems and needs will lead to a new and more satisfying regime. If this fails, or if a neutral counsellor would help to break the ice, it is worth pursuing this line. This is a relatively new area of expertise and your doctor, the Family Planning Association or Marriage Guidance Council will give advice on who to consult. Whoever you go to will certainly want to see both of you, separately and together. You should not give up without a good honest try to get going again. Much of what you do and your attitude to it needs reappraisal and discussion in retirement. Your sex life is no exception to this but you may need to be brave to get it sorted out. Given the right approach and a high sense of well-being, this should not be difficult.

3 Keeping physically fit

I have recently completed a fascinating exercise on fifty volunteers who, in groups of ten, were offered six months, supervision at five Fitness For Industry centres in various parts of the country. Their ages varied from fifty-seven to seventy-two with most of them well over sixty. None was fit beforehand and several had medical disabilities, such as high blood pressure or moderate angina. One man had an artificial leg. The regime was moderately arduous and the early stages required much determination to continue because of the aches and pains.

The object was to measure physical improvement and also get some idea as to its possible benefits. Virtually all of them, men and women, showed measurable improvement in strength, pulse rate, oxygen utilisation and, in some cases, reduction in blood pressure. They all felt significantly better and more lively, and several lost many of their previous aches and pains. Most of the people promised to keep it up in one way or another, but the most impressive factor was that they all felt so much better and were able to do more in the rest of their day. Each group also developed great supportive solidarity and the exercise developed into a social support group, perhaps partly replacing the loss of association with work. In medical terms, we also demonstrated significant improvement in symptoms like angina or a reduction in drugs required. Most people slept better.

It is difficult to prove statistically a relationship between physical fitness, well-being and effectiveness, but it is reasonable to assume that this exists for most of us. Rare beings will proclaim that they survive because they lie down when activity is mooted but for most of us reasonable physical fitness, particularly as one get older, is a sensible discipline. In physiological terms, muscles exist to be used and joints to be regularly flexed. Without this, joints creak like a rusty gate with unused hinges and muscles become flabby. It is easier to keep up muscle strength by regular use than to restore weakness that has been acquired by disease and disuse. This means that about half an hour a day, as a minimum, should be spent taking brisk exercise (even going up and down stairs in a block of flats in bad weather). The heart muscle comes in to this. It has to be kept fit and have a reserve by being made to cope with getting out of breath. This is why patients who have had a coronary thrombosis or heart operation are now sent to a supervised gymnasium.

One of the stereotypes of getting older is that one becomes weaker. This is largely untrue, you can go on being strong if you use your muscles regularly. What is required is two separate regimes: the first to maintain mobility and flexibility by bending and stretching exercise; the second to develop and then maintain strength by aerobic exercise producing mild breathlessness. There is no ideal way to do this. Anything is better than nothing and it is never too late to start. In spite of what some doctors say, there are few medical disabilities that preclude some sort of exercise. The words 'you are getting older, you must take is easy' should be banned from medical parlance. Your body will tell you when it has had enough and if you do a little more every day it is surprising, and encouraging, how much you improve.

The important thing is to do what you enjoy most or dislike least: walking, jogging, dancing, swimming, gardening and so on. There is also an increasing number of fitness centres which offer supervision and encouragement with special sessions for retired people. Swimming, if available, is good for older people because it is non-weight bearing and uses all the muscle groups.

I have purposely not gone into details of exercise and fitness schedules because there are so many available. I would, however, mention the *BUPA Book of Fitness and Wellbeing* published by Macdonalds (October 1984). This gives details of individual exercises and a range of aerobic activities and sports. Each section is age and sex rated so that anyone can slot themselves into a regime. As the editor, I say with due modesty that much in this book will help and encourage older people to live sensibly.

Included in any fitness exhortation is the question of weight. Life insurance companies discovered many years ago that thin people live longer than fat ones. More important in later life is the simple fact that the less there is of you to cart around, the easier it is. Equally if there is a bit of arthritis, bad back, hip or knee, it is essential to minimise the load on this, by weight reduction. In spite of disability it is essential to keep mobile.

Reasonable physical fitness has five benefits:

- you are likely to live longer
- you will feel better
- you will perform better and have more general energy
- you will feel virtuous about it and, provided you don't become a bore, it is legitimate
- you will sleep better.

It is never too late to start and there is always room for improvement.

Arthritis, rheumatism and mobility

Rheumatism is a diagnosis beloved by doctors and accepted by patients. Used loosely, it refers to a non-existent disease but becomes a useful dumping ground for the various aches, pains and twinges that beset us all. These have a multitude of real and imagined causes and it is not the purpose of this section to go into them in detail except to say that any cure that works is legitimate. Fringe treatments like osteopathy, manipulation, acupuncture and so on may well be better than 'proper' medicine.

Rheumatoid arthritis, on the other hand, is very much a disease, involving inflammation of the tissues around joints and destruction of the joints themselves. It is a destructive disease, tending to be more common in women. Its cause is unknown and there is a range of treatments, some of which work some of the time. I believe it to have a large stress element but not everyone will agree. It is dealt with by rheumatologists.

Rehabilitation from injury, disability and strokes, as well as rheumatoid arthritis, is dealt with by specialists in physical medicine, who are not always the same as rheumatologists, and physiotherapists. Orthopaedic specialists are surgeon carpenters who deal with injury, deformity and bone disease. Clearly there is some overlap in these three groups and neurosurgeons also get in on the act when nerves are involved — as they often are in prolapsed discs.

Osteo-arthritis, or arthritis for short, is a wear-and-tear disease of joints in which the protective cartilage over bone ends gets eroded and pain results. It also follows injury or infection. Obviously it is more common in older people, worse in the overweight and may result from overload or compensation. Thus, a bad back, old knee injury or a short leg, leading to years of compensation to get both feet on the ground or keep your head straight, puts a strain on other muscles and joints which finally rebel and become painful and arthritic.

It is also a fact of physiology that if a joint, like the knee, becomes injured or swollen, the muscles surrounding it become weak because the pain stops them being used. A vicious circle is set up because weak muscles lead to more injury. This is particularly true of back pain when an original injury, perhaps treated by a belt or brace, leads to weak muscles. The back then becomes vulnerable and continues to be over-protected, creating another vicious circle. It is therefore essential to keep up muscle strength by regular special exercises to maintain tone and mobility.

There is another point related to mobility and that is the danger to older people of falling over. When I worked in a busy casualty department after the war we used to know that on a slippery night we would get our quota of broken wrists and hips. Bones, particularly in women, become more brittle with age and hence more fragile. The sense of balance and ability to react quickly also diminish. If you do have a mobility problem or it is slippery, don't be too proud to use a stick, which can be the greatest help. It must be strong enough, have a good handle and a rubber tip. Above all, it must be the right length so that it will take your weight with the arm more or less straight.

To summarise, physical stimulation is essential to maintain liveliness. Muscles and joints must be used regularly in winter and summer to the extent of producing mild breathlessness. Any form of exercise will do but swimming is recommended for older people. Strength only diminishes with age because of disuse. It is never too late to start. Try getting a medium sized dog and take it out yourself. I can promise that the relatively sedentary who get themselves fitter will feel much better. Age is little barrier to many games, if played with peers and not tyros.

Keeping in good trim

Most of the points about maintaining your well-being have already been made and you should have started investing in your health in middle age. I am a strong protagonist of the health check and regard this as preventive maintenance on people. It is like having your car serviced. Early changes can be picked up and dealt with, and life style problems dicussed. It seems to me to be sensible to keep this up although the procedures need not be so extensive as at a BUPA centre. Sadly, the NHS is not prevention oriented but some GPs and group practices do offer simple health checks and if you can afford it one of the specialist centres will be pleased to go on seeing you. It is wise to have hearing, vision, blood pressure, blood and urine checked every year or eighteen months, largely to ensure that there has been no change and that insidious diseases like diabetes have not crept in.

Older people expect to get a bit stiff and less mobile and if they have a long standing disability, like deafness or a bone deformity, they expect it to get worse. Similarly many GPs may label someone a diabetic or whatever and tend not to look for other conditions. I think it wise to seek expert advice every two or three years about any disability. After all, the state of the art may have changed and new treatments become available, so do try to get a regular simple health check.

Warning signs and symptoms

I make the point in the special section for women (see page 63) that you control your own medical destiny. Doctors, sadly, never seek out their patients to see how they are. This is something which they ought to do for their older ones. It rests with you, therefore, to report any changes or discuss any anxieties.

Dealing with most diseases, particularly cancer, depends on early diagnosis. This in turn depends on the patient reporting early to the doctor who then has to clutch at straws and make sure that the symptoms are not significant. It is always up to the patient to report to the doctor and not put it off because he does not want to bother him. Doctors are there to be bothered — legitimately and sensibly — and to bother about their patients.

Any change or set of symptoms which lasts for more than a fortnight should be reported. The main changes to look out for are:

● Loss of weight and appetite.
● Great gain in weight without dietary over-indulgence.
● Persistent headache.
● Change in sleep pattern, waking early and feeling gloomy. Depression is common, treatable and often missed. Tranquillisers and sleeping pills do not help.
● Breathlessness, persistent cough and swollen ankles at the end of the day. A mild degree of ankle swelling which has gone by the morning is almost normal.
● Any bleeding from anywhere, from coughing, vomiting, rectum or vagina, must be reported at once.
● Any bleeding or pain from a skin lesion or change in the size or appearance of an established mole or skin blemish: report at once.
● Change of bowel habit or difficulty. This can be looseness or constipation, or alternate. Most bowel cancers present like this, with pain, discharge or discomfort. If caught early they respond well to surgery.
● Any pain anywhere which is new and persists for more than a few days, particularly if it is not related to an injury.
● New lumps or bumps that you can see or feel even if they are painless. 'Old friends' are safe to leave provided they don't change.
● Pain in the leg or chest on walking or exercise.

The list could be endless but these are the main signals. What it adds up to is to be sensible about any new symptoms. Don't hope that they will go away, but get a check on them. Most will turn out to be harmless but it is very much a case of a stitch in time. The onus for threading the needle rests on you.

Diet and digestion

We live at a time when fashion and exhortation about diet is rampant and it must be difficult for the average person to keep a sense of perspective in the face of conflicting advice. There are, however, two main threads running through this tangle.

The first is to keep your weight within reasonable limits, roughly within 10 per cent of optimum. For most people this is purely a matter of calorie book-keeping. If you eat more calories than are required for daily life, these are banked as fat. Thus the overweight person on a steady diet ticks over with a large credit account. Eating is very much a matter of habit, and of family and cultural group behaviour, so that eating patterns tend to be rigid and passed on through the children. Some of us are better converters than others and have to be careful. Others, the thin active ectomorphs, can eat what they like and never put on weight.

The second and more important thread is the need to reduce the toll of coronary heart disease which, although dropping in the USA, is still static and high in this country. Coronary heart disease is multi-factorial in its causes but diet, in particular the fat content, is undoubtedly important. In developed countries the consumption of animal fats and dairy products has increased since the war, so too have the average weights of the population. Obesity has been called the commonest disease and we do all tend to suffer from over-nutrition. For good reasons there is now considerable pressure, supported by the government and their expert advisers, to get back to a more 'natural' diet. This is not organic food, for there is no hard evidence of the benefits of this, but a more fibre-rich diet with fruit, vegetables and wholemeal products and much less meat and dairy products. This does have nutritional advantages but obviously conflicts with the farming lobby and EEC policy. The human digestive system is designed to function on bulk and it does need a good volume of roughage to push through, particularly as it gets older and less flexible.

Another trend, especially for single people and small families, is to be tempted by packaged, convenience foods. Although often tasty, they have, by definition, to be short of fibre or low in residue.

What this boils down to for older people is to eat more or less what you like provided that you keep your weight at a reasonable level. Bearing in mind the need for regular exercise, it is easier to achieve this without having too much weight to cart around. After retirement, the load on an inevitably ageing system, bones, joints, and muscles as well as the heart should be minimised to reduce wear and tear.

I have found over my clinical years that many older people do tend to experience bowel trouble. This is often miraculously improved by a modest increase in fibre — taking bran cereal for breakfast, for example. I believe too that the human engine is designed for regular feeding and likes three meals a day, but they need not be heavy ones. Age on the whole demands simpler food at regular times with plenty of fruit, vegetables and fibre and not too much animal fat.

If you have a digestive problem, perhaps an old ulcer (although these are now much less common), hiatus hernia or difficult colon, it is likely to improve with retirement and lessening tension. The digestive system is particularly prone to stress and anxiety and usually improves on holiday and in retirement. But if this does not happen in, say, three months, you should see your doctor and have it re-investigated.

Fluid intake becomes more important with age. The kidneys function less well and lose some of their power of concentration. This means more dilute urine will be produced which, coupled with a weaker bladder, means getting up at night. This encourages a tendency to cut down on fluids towards the end of the day which is not sensible. Fluid intake should be kept up at about three pints a day and more in hot weather. Mild dehydration, which must be avoided, does throw an increased load on the circulation and may even precipitate a minor stroke. On the whole it does not matter what fluid is taken but tea or coffee with sugar is a high calorie food and so is alcohol. I am strongly in favour of alcohol in moderation and there is no reason to stop it in retirement. In fact, if you are likely to become alcohol dependent, this will probably have happened already — which is a different problem. But I have known people retiring unsuccessfully, ie without thinking through the problems and making sensible plans, to become depressed and start drinking too much. This obviously has to be guarded against.

Many of my patients have found that their alcohol tolerance diminishes as they get older and that suddenly there are certain drinks they can no longer take. Sadly this is probably a function of an ageing digestion and less efficient liver. The liver has to work quite hard dealing with alcohol and the enzyme systems involved work more slowly. Little can be done to help this except to experiment with various drinks, to take them with meals and in a not too concentrated form. Dry Martinis and brandy may sadly be out.

Salt

There is currently a great deal of controversy about the possible role of salt in the causation of high blood pressure. My own feeling is that it will finally be shown to be an important piece of what is a complicated jigsaw. Again, this is a disease which is multi-factorial. There is a growing volume of evidence to suggest that reduction or elimination of salt will reduce raised blood pressure and also the strength of the drugs required to lower it. This is not, however, to say that too much salt in the normal diet caused the condition in the first place, but for some types of hypertension it could have played a part.

Salt has little nutritional value and is taken largely as a matter of taste and habit. We have all become used to food containing a lot of salt. It is also included in most processed food and dressings. When I was last in America visiting a coronary rehabilitation unit, the doctors complained bitterly that there were no regulations requiring the salt content of processed food to be given on the packet and that it was impossible to buy salt-free products.

It does seem that it would be sensible, and no great hardship, if we all got used to using less salt in our diets (and for once there would be no great socio-economic implications). In the meantime, if you have a blood pressure problem your doctor will advise you about how much salt to take and in any case it would be wise to cut down on extra salt.

Retirement is all about enjoyment but with discipline. Eating and drinking are major pleasures and should continue to be indulged. If you retire in reasonable health you are unlikely to be an immediate coronary candidate and need not worry too much about diet, provided your weight is controlled, enough fibre is taken and fluid intake is kept up.

4 Seeing and hearing

Sight

Most of us require glasses for reading some time in middle age. As the eye gets older the lens and its supporting mechanism loses its elasticity. The eye focuses from distance to near sight by relaxing the lens to alter its focal length. Loss of elasticity means that the near point recedes and small print cannot been seen clearly. As people say, 'my arms are not long enough', and the receding print is then too small.

Reading glasses are merely simple plus lenses which magnify the subject. It is, however, important to continue having your eyes tested regularly and to have the right glasses. If you do fine work at a distance different from comfortable reading, it is often sensible to get a pair of specific glasses for this activity.

Short-sighted people go through the same age change which means that their near point retreats in the same way. Thus they need less strong concave lenses and may in fact manage without any at all. They tend to think that their eyes are getting better.

Astigmatism is due to irregularity of the surface of the eye giving distorted vision. This does not change much with age so that the same correction has to be built into any reading or other glasses.

What is not so generally realised is that the ageing eye requires much more light to see efficiently. Most domestic lighting tends to be on the dim side and there is a strong case for retirement planning to include a good pool of light, perhaps an anglepoise for each member of the house. For the same reasons it is wise to review the lighting in kitchens and corridors to minimise accidents and increase efficiency. Put a new light over the stove, the sink and the back door. Accidents account for a lot of disability in the elderly.

Cataract, which is a gradually developing opacity in the lens, is common in older people. It is now much easier to deal with, either by removal or a plastic lens implant. If removed, strong glasses are needed to replace the lens itself and here contact lenses can be a help.

Glaucoma is the commonest cause of blindness in older people. It is due to failure of the drainage system within the eye. Pressure builds up and does the eye no good at all. It tends to be a familial condition and can be acute or chronic. Any pain in the eye, sudden frontal headache or vomiting associated with pain, should be reported at once as a medical emergency because a sudden rise in pressure can cause blindness.

Vision is far too precious to take risks with and although eye strain is a myth, it is prudent to get expert advice. Opticians are good at eye testing and prescribing glasses and there is now direct access to them on the NHS. However older people in particular ought to see an eye specialist if there are difficulties not dealt with by simple reading glasses.

If you want more information about eyes and vision, there is an admirable book, *Eyes — Their Problems and Treatments* by Dr Michael Glasspool, published in the Martin Dunitz Positive Health Series (in fact, the whole series is an excellent source of medical and health information).

Hearing

Although age-related sight changes are accepted and understood and glasses are socially acceptable, it is not generally realised that hearing deteriorates in the same way. The problem is therefore dealt with at some length here, by reproducing — with kind permission of the authors and publisher — two excellent articles on hearing and, specifically, tinnitus, by Dafydd Stephens and Lorraine Jeffrey Nicol of the Audiology Centre, Royal National Throat, Nose and Ear Hospital in London. These were first published in *Choice* magazine.

Better hearing for the elderly

by Dafydd Stephens and Lorraine Jeffrey Nicol

Introduction

Recent studies by the Medical Research Council's Institute of Hearing Research have shown that about one in four of the adult population of this country complain of hearing difficulties and one in six have significant noises in their ears. The likelihood of having hearing difficulties increases markedly with age, so that only four per cent of twenty year olds have hearing problems, whereas twenty-five per cent of seventy year olds have such difficulties, the percentage increasing in even older people.

A somewhat similar pattern occurs with noises in the ears (or tinnitus), some six per cent of people aged about twenty years having this problem and fifteen per cent of those aged about seventy. A further important fact concerning hearing loss is that mild to moderate hearing losses are far more common than severe losses. Complete deafness is very rare amongst those not born deaf and the average elderly person with hearing problems is generally only moderately hard of hearing.

One of the problems, and perhaps blessings, of most hearing loss in middle aged and elderly people is that it comes on very gradually, causing insidiously increasing difficulties. Consequently an individual suffering from a hearing loss may not be aware that they are having problems, until perhaps someone draws attention to the fact that they:

- no longer hear the telephone and/or doorbell every time they ring;
- need to have the volume of the television or radio at a level which others may find either uncomfortable or annoying; and
- are unable to follow a group conversation with ease.

The gradual onset of hearing loss is only partly responsible for individuals attending an audiology centre for the first time having experienced difficulties for some fifteen years. A further contributory factor is that some of the 'deaf is daft' myth still persists and fuels the social stigma associated with hearing loss and hearing aids.

It is very important to act on your hearing problems as soon as you begin to experience them; a delay in doing so can result in increased difficulties in handling a hearing aid and learning new listening skills. The handling problems may be related to arthritis, stroke, tremor (shaking) or loss of sensitivity in the fingers. The likelihood of someone having any of these problems increases markedly with age. In a recent study on handling skills of people fitted with hearing aids, we found that none of those first fitted in their sixties had serious problems. However, among those fitted for the first time in their eighties, only a third had no real problems. Furthermore, certain causes of hearing loss may be reversible if treated early but are certainly not if left a long time. The importance of acting quickly cannot be stressed enough. Indeed, would you wait fifteen years from the time you begin to have difficulty reading a newspaper before going to visit an optician or ophthalmologist?

What to do if you have hearing problems

What steps then should you take if and when you begin to experience hearing problems and/or persistent or recurrent noises in the ears?

First, you should take advice from your GP. He or she should be able to define whether or not your hearing problems/noises are due to a reasonably treatable condition, whether they could possibly be related to something sinister (very rarely) or whether you require rehabilitative help. In the vast majority of cases, your GP would generally take further advice from an audiological physician or ENT surgeon, except in those whose problems are due to easily treatable causes. In addition, under the present organisation of the NHS, most of the hearing rehabilitative services are based in the hospitals where such specialists are found.

In such a centre, you will probably find that there is no medical/surgical treatment for your difficulties and what you will need is appropriate rehabilitation. While hearing aids will generally play a central role in such rehabilitation, as they constitute the only reasonable form of wearable amplification, there are additional and alternative approaches to helping with certain of the problems arising from hearing loss. The rehabilitative process should be orientated towards solving the problems (disabilities and handicaps) arising from your hearing loss, rather than trying to match a hearing aid to the hearing loss measure. Indeed, in most cases of hearing loss a hearing aid will never restore 'normal' hearing because of the damage to the inner ear (the most common site of hearing loss) resulting in a variety of distortions which cannot be overcome by current electronic technology.

This said, it is important to repeat that hearing aids play a unique part in the rehabilitative process, particularly in communication situations.

Hearing aids

Staying for a moment with hearing aids, it is worth considering the various types currently available. Within the NHS, there is now quite a comprehensive range of behind-the-ear hearing aids, several body-worn aids and a few ear trumpets which still have a limited but useful role. In addition, there are spectacle adaptors for many of the behind-the-ear aids so that, with the aid of your optician, they may be fitted to spectacle frames. This is obviously relevant if you wear one pair of spectacles all the time.

Everyone will have seen advertisements in the popular press for in-the-ear and in-the-canal hearing aids aimed at the need felt by many people to hide their hearing loss and hearing aid. Some of these aids made and fitted by reputable companies do have undoubted acoustical as well as cosmetic advantages. The major drawback of these devices, apart from the fact that they are not normally available on the NHS, is that their controls are very small and difficult to handle for many elderly people, and they may be difficult for them to fit into their ears. Furthermore, most of those currently produced are made, as far as that is possible, to match the individual's hearing loss, so that it is difficult to change their characteristics as the listener adapts to his or her new listening situation or as their hearing changes.

Certain advertisements for 'hearing correctors' with no electronics are frankly misleading. Their only role is in those people with floppy ear canals which are held open by such devices. This is a rare cause of significant hearing loss and the benefit which most people can obtain from such devices is nil.

In the choice or acceptance of any hearing aid or aids it is essential that you, the user, should be able to handle the controls adequately, change the batteries without any problem and fit the earmould into your ear. This last is one of the commonest causes of difficulty among the elderly and it is important that you should ensure that the person fitting the hearing aid gives you adequate training and practice at such fitting. If, after much demonstration and practice, it still proves to be impossible, alternative approaches to wearable amplification should be considered. These include using the hearing aid with a stetoclip, as used by tape typists, or possibly using a device recently come onto the market for less than £20 — a 'listening aid' based on a walkman type amplifier with two-directional microphones going to a stereo headset.

Other aids to hearing

For many people who can manage well in the communication situations which they encounter in their daily life, but have other particular difficulties, so called 'environmental aids' may be more useful than hearing aids. These may also be used to supplement hearing aids in those people who use the latter.

Environmental aids are not provided through the NHS but may be obtained from the Social Service Departments by people who register with them as 'hard of hearing'. Unfortunately, provisions throughout the country are somewhat variable due to the fact that they come under the non-mandatory provisions of the Chronically Sick and Disabled Persons Act.

Environmental aids may be divided into those which provide additional or alternative amplification, and those which provide alerting and warning signals. A variety of such devices was described in the *Which?* magazine, October 1981, and also in various leaflets produced by the Royal National Institute for the Deaf (RNID), 105 Gower Street, London WC1. The RNID also produces a regular newsletter, *Soundbarrier*, full of news on these and other items, together with many helpful articles.

The additional amplification may be applied to telephones, with amplifying headsets, couplers to link them to hearing aids, inductaphones built into the telephone for the same purpose, and additional receivers. A variety of additional amplifier devices is available for television and radio listening with personalised headsets, additional loudspeakers, loop systems and the like.

Alert and warning devices help with problems in hearing the doorbell and the telephone bell when you are not close to them. These may range from extension bells or extra loud bells to systems which flash the lights on and off. A variety of devices are also available for replacing the quiet alarm clock with extra loud systems, flashing light devices or vibrators under the pillow.

In all cases, it is important to consult your Social Service Department or the RNID first, even if you intend to buy such devices yourself, as they can advise you as to what is most appropriate for your needs. In addition, an increasing number of audiology and hearing aid departments have displays of such devices and, in particular, the hearing therapists there (if you have one in your area) usually have knowledge and experience of them.

In many places, hearing therapists or other health care professionals organise communication training, which may be on an individual or group basis. This covers both hearing tactics, lipreading skills, listening skills and advice with other problems.

Lipreading classes or groups may be useful as long as you do not expect them to transform you from a hopeless lipreader into an expert. The chances are, indeed, that you are already a good lipreader without being aware of it. The real importance of such groups is that you can learn much from how other people have overcome their hearing problems, come to realise that you are not alone with your difficulties, and learn many ways in which you can make communication easier for yourself.

Conclusions

Overall, the main point is not to be ashamed of your hearing difficulty; it is very common and you should not try to hide it. Indeed, a major hearing aid manufacturer produced a very good poster which said 'Hearing aids are less conspicuous than poor hearing'. Do not pretend that you can hear. You cannot fool most people. Consult your doctor as soon as you are aware of persistent hearing problems, even if only in one ear, and obtain appropriate professional advice to help you deal with the problem from audiology/ENT centres and from your Social Services.

Once you have done this, you may find that some of the local facilities are inadequate, in health and social service provisions, in places of entertainment and in places of work. It is only by drawing this to the attention of the people responsible, and if they are unable to do anything about it, bringing in your local councillors and MPs, that such provisions will be improved.

Tinnitus

by Dafydd Stephens and Lorraine Jeffrey Nicol

Introduction

Tinnitus is the sensation of sound/s in the ear, ears or head in the absence of external sounds. In most cases this is heard only by the individual concerned, but in a few rare cases, using listening tubes or electronic systems, other people may be able to hear the tinnitus. The sound or sounds heard may be of all types, ringing, whistling, churring, hissing or a great variety of complex sounds or combination of sounds. However, if 'normal' individuals are put in a soundproof room for a long period of time, they will all experience tinnitus equivalent to that reported by patients suffering from the symptom.

Tinnitus is a symptom generally indicating some damage to the inner ear or to other parts of the auditory system. It is a very common symptom experienced from time to time by at least one-third of the adult population. Recent studies have shown that about one in six of the adult population experience tinnitus lasting more than a few minutes. However, only about one in twenty-five of the adult population find it annoying and one per cent or less are seriously disturbed by it. Tinnitus is generally associated with some hearing loss, and because the occurrence of hearing loss increases dramatically with age, the likelihood of anyone experiencing tinnitus also increases significantly in the elderly.

What should you do if you have tinnitus?

If the tinnitus persists more than a few days, especially if it is occurring in one ear, you should consult your general practitioner about it. It commonly occurs after fevers, such as influenza, after exposure to loud noises, with impacted wax in the ear and in certain middle ear conditions. These generally tend to settle by themselves or may be treatable by your general practitioner or by an appropriate specialist.

It is, however, worth mentioning that those who have been exposed to considerable noise at work, in the armed forces or otherwise, are much more likely to suffer from tinnitus subsequently than those who have not been exposed to such noise. It is therefore advisable, if you use power tools for DIY activities, to use some kind of hearing protection such as earplugs or ear muffs as a preventative measure.

If your tinnitus does not settle by itself or with this treatment, your GP will refer you to an audiological physician or ENT surgeon who will have the facilities to investigate your problem further and arrange appropriate treatment of the underlying cause if it is amenable to such treatment.

It must, however, be emphasised that in many individuals, either the cause of the tinnitus has been in the past, such as noise exposure, head injury or a hereditary condition, so that there is no continuing condition to be treated or, alternatively, it is impossible to identify a cause despite extensive investigation. In this case, the specialist must turn to symptomatic treatment.

Symptomatic treatment of tinnitus

First, it must be stated that there is no universal 'cure' for tinnitus. Most treatments are aimed at helping the patient to accept and get used to the symptom and to relieve the problems secondary to the tinnitus, such as sleep disturbance, anxiety, depression and listening difficulties.

We all tend to imagine that any symptom is an indication of sinister disease, and adequate investigation to provide reassurance helps us to accept any persistent symptom much more easily. Excessive anxiety will tend to enhance the symptom and if the individual ceases to be frightened, this in itself will be therapeutic. Indeed, the normal process with people suffering from tinnitus is to learn to accept their tinnitus and to cease to worry about it although this may take a different length of time for different people and with different patterns of tinnitus.

For those who have difficulties in getting used to their tinnitus, there are three main lines of approach — psychological, acoustical and pharmacological — with more drastic and destructive approaches such as surgery being restricted to the more severe cases, resistant to all other approaches.

Acoustical management

In the majority of people with tinnitus who also have a hearing loss, the first line of approach should be to help their hearing loss with a hearing aid. These have a threefold effect, reducing the amount that the individual has to strain to hear and hence strain to hear through his tinnitus; masking or blotting out the tinnitus with external sounds; and introducing extraneous sounds which distract the individual from his tinnitus. This may be supplemented by introducing more distracting sounds into the most quiet environments, for example, the bedroom such as by replacing the digital alarm clock with a noisy, old-fashioned clock. This approach is valuable for most sufferers. If it results in insufficient masking or distraction, it may be worth trying a tinnitus masker. This is basically a noise generator built into a hearing aid case, which produces a sound which masks out the tinnitus, provides a relief from the particular sound of the tinnitus and puts the loudness of the sound going into the individual's ears under his own control. Many patients find these invaluable but in others they are less effective.

Psychological management

The theory behind this is to stop the individual worrying about his tinnitus and to help him to learn to live with it. Various techniques have been used, including biofeedback, relaxation training and cognitive therapy, with good results. They lead to a reduction in the annoyance caused by the tinnitus but not in its loudness. Such an approach may also have a dramatic effect on the secondary symptoms provoked by the tinnitus.

Pharmacological management

Only one drug, Lignocaine, has been shown to be consistently effective in actually suppressing tinnitus in a majority of sufferers, but unfortunately that can only be taken by injection into the veins, and even then the effect usually lasts only a few minutes. Much research is taking place to find more effective equivalents which can be taken by mouth, but at the moment there is no dramatic cure.

Other drugs may be used to overcome some of the problems which some individuals may have secondary to the tinnitus, such as difficulties in getting to sleep, early waking, depression and general tenseness. These are the drugs used for such conditions in other more general circumstances.

Conclusions

Tinnitus is a very common symptom and is due to a variety of causes, many of which are not amenable to simple treatment. The normal situation is that sufferers get to accept their tinnitus. Should such acceptance not occur, despite reassurance, a variety of psychological, acoustical and pharmacological approaches are available for use, individually or in combination, which can help this process in the majority of sufferers. There is no magical cure for the symptom.

Teeth

by K J Lewis, FDS

A major part of the preventative philosophy that has grown within the dental profession over the past twenty years is that teeth should be saved whenever possible. Since most tooth extractions are for patients in their forties and fifties, the benefits for the over forties are self evident.

More teeth are extracted as a result of gum disease than because of dental decay. Because of new techniques and materials, today's dental surgeon has a wide range of options to transform even the most painful and hopeless looking 'shells' of what were once recognisable teeth, into comfortable and functional teeth again; indistinguishable from the originals, provided that the gums themselves and — more important — the underlying *bone* are adequate to support them.

Let us backtrack a decade or so and consider what kind of problems are being faced by the average fifty year old today.

First, you will probably have teeth, and many of them. These teeth arrived in the mouth soon after the NHS was getting under way, so in a sense they were luckier than they might have been had their owner been born ten or fifteen years earlier. The familiar story is that they received, first, some small fillings, and later these were replaced by larger fillings and then a succession of progressively larger fillings over the years until you wonder whether it is only the dentist's willpower that's holding them together. More extensively repaired teeth may have been graced by inlays, crowns or bridges. Some of the teeth may be a little looser in their sockets than they were, or painful to bite hard upon. The gums may bleed when you brush your teeth, or the gums may have receded round the necks of the teeth, exposing sensitive root tissue. If the very thought of a mouthful of ice-cream sends you skywards, or perhaps even the physical act of toothbrushing is painful in these areas, take heart because such problems are usually manageable. It is important to recognise the warning signs, seek professional advice from a dental surgeon and take stock of the situation.

Whatever your age, reflect on the state of your mouth ten years ago, five years ago, two years ago and today. Are things pretty much as they were or are you going downhill fast? Have you lost any teeth over this period? Have you had a succession of problems with specific teeth, and have these been satisfactorily resolved? Has your dentist expressed any kind of doubt as to the long-term survival of your remaining teeth, or given you any general feeling that he is trying to 'let you down slowly' without giving you any specific reason or explanation? Perhaps he is an old friend as well as a trusted professional advisor and the only response you have elicited from him is a silently raised eyebrow of pleasant surprise to see so many gnarled old friends still present at the routine check-up, before you exchange the usual social pleasantries. It is a good friend indeed who can put frankness above friendliness and give you sound professional advice in between the laughing and joking.

What you really need, of course, is an honest opinion of your dental and oral health — where you are now and where you are going. If in doubt, don't be afraid to seek a second opinion either from another dentist in general practice or from a consultant.

It is reasonable to suppose that there will be consultant dental surgeons just as there are consultant gynaecologists, eye specialists or whatever; after all, the mouth is a pretty small place and the teeth but one part of it. Surprisingly, there are no fewer than seven major clinical specialities within dentistry itself, not to mention scores more non-clinical specialities, with consultants for every one of them. A consultant in one branch of dentistry has highly specialised skills often remote from those of another branch of dentistry, and in true medical fashion they have confusing titles. When seeking an opinion you obviously need to approach the correct consultant. The ones that will concern you most are:

(1)   Periodontics/periontology — gums.
(2)   Conservative dentistry — natural teeth, fillings, crowns, bridges etc. This includes endodontics, ie 'root-filling' of teeth.
(3)   Prosthetic dentistry — partial and complete dentures, ie the replacement of missing teeth other than by crowns and bridges etc.
(4)   Restorative dentistry — this is a relatively new and growing group of consultants, who are already consultants in at least one of the above three specialities and whose skill and knowledge will probably encompass all of them anyway. They are thus able to give a broader evaluation.

Most of these consultants are located in the main teaching hospitals and dental schools which are found in the larger cities. In the provinces, the consultant at the local district or general hospital will normally be a consultant in oral and maxillofacial surgery (dealing with complex disorders of the mouth and jaws, tumours, fractures etc) or in orthodontics (straightening children's teeth), neither of which should be what you are looking for, but there are a few exceptions around the country which you should now be able to confirm for yourself.

If you want to keep your teeth, you need to find a general practitioner who shares your ambitions, and preferably one whose philosophy of preventative dentistry encompasses the special problems of the older patient. Many of these focus on maintaining the health of the supporting tissues of the teeth — the gums, the underlying bone and the tissues attaching the tooth root to the bone. Treatment should certainly include plenty of practical advice at regular intervals on how to clean your teeth as thoroughly as possible.

This may sound a little like trying to tell granny how to suck eggs, and indeed it can be an unexpected and embarrassing shock later in life to be sat down by somebody young enough to be your granddaughter and be given a lesson in toothbrushing. Most preventative practices now employ dental hygienists; they have been given particular training in their field and their qualification recognises these special skills in the field of dental hygiene. This includes the scaling and polishing of teeth, with various associated techniques, together with dental health education. They also carry out a range of special preventative procedures for children.

The professional cleaning of teeth (scale and polish) is an undervalued and misunderstood procedure. You may know that scale (also known as *calculus* or *tartar*) forms a hard yellowish film on the surface of the lower front teeth. It develops from the invisible sticky film of bacteria called dental plaque which forms in our mouths all day, every day. Unfortunately, the same layer forms *under* the gum where it is invisible and it is here that it helps to cause gum disease unless removed, by providing a hiding place for more plaque. A scaling that simply removes the obvious deposits above the gum and polishes the teeth so that they feel smooth and shiny has really served little or no useful purpose. A hygienist is not a kind of second-class dentist — instead, he or she has been trained to carry out one small part of the dentist's work to a high degree of skill — an important distinction.

When a hygienist or a dental health educator, another kind of ancillary specialist in the modern dental practice, suggests new and unfamiliar ways of cleaning your teeth it is for a good reason. First, your mouth presents a different kind of cleaning problem every time a new filling, crown, bridge or denture is placed and — more surprisingly, perhaps — the teeth do move within the jaws from year to year and indeed from month to month, presenting new and different problems. It is as illogical to expect one toothbrushing routine to last forever as it is to expect the curtains in one house to fit another. Shapes and sizes are obviously different. Similarly, what is right for one patient can be inappropriate for another. So it is with the teeth

and gums, and advice on toothbrushing should be on a continuing personal basis, adjusting to changing circumstances,
and certainly not a once-and-for-all litany as many people
believe.

There are various techniques such as the strengthening or supporting of the remaining teeth with pins, screws or cast posts,
crowns, bridges, splints and precision attachments, but for
those readers who may have but a few teeth remaining, or
even none at all, I must say a word about dentures.

The simplest form of partial denture is the pink or clear plastic
plate, carrying plastic artificial teeth. When you bite on this
denture much of the force is transmitted to the gum and soft
tissues underneath — tissues which are ill-equipped to tolerate
such abuse. While the palate, for example, is well supported
on bone and capable of accepting these loads, the gum certainly isn't and this, together with the plaque that plastic dentures tend to harbour, can cause rapid deterioration in the
health of the gum beneath them.

Metal 'skeleton' dentures — previously made of stainless steel
but now normally chrome-cobalt, are not only stronger, but
smaller, lighter and less bulky. They cover much less gum tissue and hence are easier to clean and, most importantly, they
are shaped to rest upon the tooth surface, with small clasps
carefully positioned to keep the denture in place. The dentist
carefully designs these dentures so that when you bite on them
selected *teeth* take these biting forces, which is precisely what
nature has equipped them to do, thus the gums stay much
healthier with this type of denture.

A variation on this theme is overdentures — an old technique
now enjoying something of a revival. This usually involves
'root-filling' the roots of various teeth, cutting the remaining
teeth down to about gum level and making a denture to sit
over the top of them. Such a denture is thus excellently supported and stays in place much better than the conventional
full set where no roots remain.

The final option when all the teeth and roots have departed is
the full or complete denture. Upper dentures have a head start
on lower dentures because of the availability of the palate for

support and retention. It is not uncommon to have problems with full dentures, particularly lower ones. Even if you don't, it is prudent to have dentures checked every two or three years to ensure that the underlying tissues are still healthy; dentures can also be relined to improve fit. If you have lost weight, or been ill, it may have affected the shape of your mouth and the fit of your dentures.

If you have an old, worn or battered denture that was basically comfortable before you discarded it, do try to retrieve it because your dentist can use it in a replica technique whereby he recreates the better aspects of the old denture and corrects any faults when producing a new set of dentures which often provide the best in all factors: comfort, fit and appearance.

To summarise, it is becoming the exception rather than the rule to end your days in the same toothless state in which you started them. Modern dentistry is unrecognisable from the days of your childhood, and more people can expect to keep more of their teeth longer and later in life.

Free information on dental matters is available from:
British Dental Health Foundation, 88 Gurnards Avenue, Unit 2, Fishermead, Milton Keynes, Bucks.

5 Special problem areas

Special problems — women

Just as the workaholic man is in my view vulnerable and boring
so is the 'pure housewife'. Looking after home and family is
splendid and has to be done by someone but when there is
only home and less family, I believe it to be an inadequate
occupation. Becoming an end in itself, it may be over-protec-
tive and inflexible, causing friction and perhaps sourness. I
know this is a provocative statement but I think it is a danger
area. Everyone should have outside interests and activities and
if the stairs don't get swept or the supper occasionally comes
from the take-away, so what?

So far I have said nothing about the working wife. She is doing
two demanding jobs and to manage these she has to be better
organised than her husband. Being a mother may also have to
be fitted in, which requires thought and priority. I suspect that,
given the right mix, children flourish in this more stimulating
environment. But the important point about the situation is
that it must make for a different relationship, both emotional
and financial. It will certainly be a more independent one and
perhaps be the better for it. Much more give and take will be
required to establish the ground rules and to agree priorities
which don't cause friction or jealousy. There is, too, the
danger that work will pull you in different directions with the
central relationship becoming less important, particularly if
there are no children. All these problems can be faced and
generally make for better adjusted people. The working wife
will face retirement problems more specifically than her more
domestic colleague and these have to be faced in the same way
as for the husband.

Difficulties do occur when, as they often are, retirement ages
are very different. A younger wife will probably want to go on

working after her husband, to get a pension or finish a job she thoroughly enjoys. This may well precipitate role reversal. A similar thing is happening with redundancy and men have to be more flexible. Such difficulties have to be realised well in advance and included in the contingency planning discussions. Women seem to be medically tougher than men if only because they manage to live longer in spite of the alleged hazards and strain of child bearing. The differential seems partially due to the fact that women have a much lower incidence of coronary thrombosis (CHD) in middle life. They also tolerate moderate degrees of raised blood pressure rather better. Perhaps the next few years will show a significant increase in their CHD rate, possibly because more are working and smoking cigarettes. In addition, it is probable that prolonged use of the contraceptive pill may contribute to this. Lifestyle plays a part in mortality statistics and this is shown by the sad and avoidable increase in lung cancer in women over the last ten years. It now more or less equals breast cancer as the commonest 'killer' of late middle aged women.

There are two specific medical problem areas for women. The first is gynaecological and the second concerns the breasts. This is not the place to embark on a detailed description of common gynaecological problems like uterine prolapse, fibroids, bladder troubles and so on. All I want to say is that if you have any symptoms, particularly bleeding, pain or discomfort, take them to your doctor at once. The cause is probably trivial and easily dealt with, but if not, early intervention is the key to cure.

Hysterectomy, removal of the womb, is a relatively common necessity, often for benign tumours or fibroids. It is a satisfactory operation and when properly done and sympathetically handled, should cause no interference with sexual intercourse. As with menopausal symptoms, there may be some dryness, easily dealt with by a simple lubricant jelly.

The menopause usually comes on at around fifty. It carries a vast mythology of symptoms and disabilities, nearly all of which are unnecessary. Many women drift through the 'change' with little discomfort, but if you are bothered by symptoms like hot flushes and so on, see your doctor and get some treatment, if necessary from a menopause clinic, of which there are now many about. The symptoms are due to hormone changes and can largely be controlled by hormone replacement — HRT. The vital thing is not to be put off by doctors who think you should suffer for the mortification of your flesh, but insist on treatment. Your sex life can continue for many years after the menopause. The BUPA Medical Centre has an excellent leaflet on the menopause and the book, *The Change of Life*, by Dr Barbara Evans, is admirable.

Breast cancer is still, sadly, an emotive subject and we still see patients who are too frightened to report lumps in their breast. One in about thirteen women dies of breast cancer every year. The breast, particularly as it ages, is a lumpy organ and it is cheering to note that fewer than a tenth of all lumps prove to be malignant. However, and this is critical, all lumps have to be regarded as suspicious until proved friendly by being looked at under a microscope. Experience over the past few years has shown two important things. The first is that successful treatment depends entirely on the removal of any cancer before it has spread and while it is very small. Secondly, and important from your point of view, is the fact that local excision, without the removal of the whole breast, is usually adequate. The days of extensive and mutilating surgery have largely passed.

Breast cancer is four times as common as cancer of the cervix. Thus, there is four times the case for breast screening for early diagnosis using special X-ray techniques with a small radiation dosage. It is now possible to pick up some tumours before they can be felt. Equally important, however, is self examination, taught at screening and Well Woman clinics. You are in the best position to notice any change and to report it at once. Similarly any bleeding or discharge from the nipple must be followed up, as some cancers begin in the ducts rather than in the breast tissue. I would urge every woman to go for breast screening, particularly when over the age of forty, and go every year. Teach your daughters and granddaughters to learn self examination and keep it up every month for life.

Of course the thought of cancer is frightening and so is the fear of losing a breast or being chopped about, but much worse are the risks of getting disseminated cancer. The problems and risks must be faced and openly discussed. Life without a breast is in fact perfectly tolerable, as is the loss of a leg, given the right attitude and adjustment. I know that it is easy for a man to say this but women doctors say it too. Breasts can be reconstructed by silicone implants, and special bras and bathing costumes are fairly easily obtained. Husbands are mostly sympathetic, or can be encouraged to be, so that once openness has been accepted, adjustment should not be too difficult.

In any case, never, never, neglect any lump in your breast — and if you have been successfully treated, tell all your friends about it. Cancer needs publicity about successful and early treatment if its toll is to be reduced.

The BUPA Medical Centres, of which there are now many well spread around the country, all have facilities for breast screening and there are quite a number of other Well Woman clinics. You should attend for regular screening every year. BUPA also have a good leaflet about breast disease and the Mastectomy Association gives admirable advice and support. Many larger hospitals have mastectomy counsellors to help with the problems of readjustment once you leave hospital.

If you act along the lines I have advocated, you will be playing safe and if you are unlucky enough to get a lump, relatively minor surgery should suffice. But as breast cancer is so common, it must be accepted as a not too unlikely event and dealt with by early treatment. Your life is in your hands and most cases can be treated early quite successfully.

Special problems — men

Men have fewer specific problems than women. The main medical problem is to minimise the chances of having a coronary before retiring. The various risk factors are largely life style related: stress, smoking, weight, exercise and blood fats. These have to be dealt with in middle age.

Apart from this, the only other common problem arises from the prostate. This is a gland on the base of the bladder surrounding its exit, the urethra. It has an irritating habit of enlarging late in life and causing obstruction. Prostate trouble is relatively common, causing difficulty in emptying the bladder, frequency and possibly slight incontinence. These are trying but not serious symptoms. The reason for mentioning them is to make the point that if you get symptoms, have them treated early rather than late. Once enlargement starts it goes on and builds up back pressure on the urinary system. This can do more harm than the enlargement itself and there is the risk of acute obstruction as an emergency, perhaps at a difficult time or when you are away on holiday. Prostatectomy used to be an unpleasant and tedious operation but it is now mostly done through a 'magic telescope' without any cutting. The stay in hospital is usually only a few days. The results are excellent and although it may be necessary to repeat the procedure in a few years because of less extensive removal, this too is easy. The only after effect may be sterility because the ejaculatory ducts which pass through the prostate may be destroyed. But, contrary to popular belief, this does not in any way stop sexual activity which can continue as usual. Sterility at this age should be no hardship.

Cancer of the prostate is one of the commoner cancers in men. It can produce the same symptoms as enlargement and is, on the whole, one of the more treatable cancers, mostly by drugs but sometimes surgery.

In older men, particularly, all urinary symptoms should be investigated as soon as they become noticeable.

6 Sheltered housing

When I joined the staff of the Institute of Directors in 1958 to initiate a study of the health problems of its members, a stimulating aspect of life was that the director, the late Sir Richard Powell, always encouraged the interest of his members into contributing to society as a whole. As his adviser on well-being, I became involved in a range of activities, largely concerning the problems of coping with getting older. Over the years, this has centred on the growth of the Pre-Retirement Association and the needs of the lonely and then the frail elderly through the Abbeyfield Society, with which I have worked for over twenty years. It is only just beginning to dawn on individuals and governments that because more people are living well into their eighties and nineties, there is a huge new problem of how to house these people in a way which provides reasonable independence with caring support. In Abbeyfield Society houses there are ten ladies over 100.

Another factor is that our society is still unwilling to discuss the related problems of cancer, the fear of dying from it, and the general topic of death. How do we cope with it and what should our survivors do when alone?

Your first rather traumatic contact with this problem area may well come earlier in trying to deal with very elderly relatives whose need for support can easily come to dominate the family and be a major burden for a wife who has to take on the responsibility of caring for her husband's possibly cantankerous and seemingly ungrateful mother or aunt.

As housing — supportive or sheltered — is very much part of this problem and has significant financial implications, it is relevant to include some outline advice because everyone has a different approach to the problem and family relationships and finances differ. Options in the private and public sectors are now rapidly increasing and changing for the better. Over the next two or three years, it is likely that there will be a wider range of choice, certainly in the private sector.

The commercial development of sheltered housing units of various kinds is a growth industry. Most of these units provide a flat or bungalow in a supportive enclave for a capital sum. There is then a service charge varying from the exorbitant to the reasonable but always likely to increase over time. This covers a range of needs and central provisions like meals, activities and medical care. Some of the schemes include reasonable integration with NHS social and medical services, such as home helps and district nurses.

The likely availability of this support is, however, both unpredictable and patchy, largely reflecting national well-being in terms of the availability of finance for both capital and revenue in providing buildings and staff. However, local authorities do have a statutory responsibility to provide what is called Part III accommodation for those who require care and cannot look after themselves, usually those who are frail, ill or disabled.

One of the problems in this legislative jungle is that of definition, and this arises under two headings: the first is need or degree of dependency — how much care is required and for how many hours a day or night. The second is whether this care is largely supportive and 'caring' and how much real medical and professional nursing is involved. There is thus a difficult grey area, exploited by the bureaucrats, between medical and Social Service support. This difficulty is carried through into medical insurance of the BUPA type because most schemes have a premium structure to cope with short-term illness and treatment, and not with long-term custodial or supportive care in which the doctor and his drugs play a small part.

What we are learning in the Abbeyfield Society is that caring by trained care assistants, working small homely units, is better and cheaper than using hospitals. Most people die in their own homes with district nurse support supplementing the family. But without suitable family type accommodation, it is difficult, expensive and in my view undesirable, to have individuals struggling to live alone with short visits from meals-on-wheels and a social worker. They are lonely, often short of money and bored, their circumstances are often made worse by inadequate heating. A major problem is to try to persuade such an elderly relative to move, while still active, into a more integrated environment.

Many of the traditional sheltered housing units lack sufficient integration. Although there is a warden, who may visit daily and be on call, the emphasis is on independence and not interdependence and there is much loneliness. A major problem at the moment, as yet largely unsolved except by organisations like Abbeyfield, is to provide continuity of care over a spectrum of need, from the not too frail to the very frail elderly who want to die in their own beds.

People who cannot cope with their room, dressing, toilet, eating and stairs, are said to need 'extra care' which is best given in custom built units, with proper lifts and facilities. The ideal to aim at, I think, is the Abbeyfield approach which other organisations are taking up, of an 'own room', self-furnished, in a small unit, supported by a 'house mother' providing two meals a day. Residents are there from choice, even if they are on supplementary benefit, and can come and go as they please and go away for a holiday or out for the evening. When they can no longer manage in this type of accommodation, they should be able to move into an extra care home nearby, which will look after their last lap or until hospital admission for an acute and often terminal disease is required. The number of extra care houses is increasing and other housing charities are moving in a similar direction.

Voluntary Housing Associations will mostly accommodate people who can support themselves or who require social security or other charitable support. The availability of this varies with the organisation, the locality and the regulations then in force. There is sadly an 'earnings rule' type of restriction for Supplementary Benefit but other grants, such as Constant Care, are less means tested.

Expert advice from a housing organisation or one like Care and Advice for the Elderly, may well have to be sought. Regulations do change from year to year.

Frequently, an older person's only major asset is their home which, for varying good and less good reasons, they want to keep on, although it may be far too big and expensive. Schemes have now been developed to capitalise this asset and use the money to support residence in sheltered housing, with the reversion at death to the estate, of any residual surplus. This is very much part of late financial planning.

About twenty years ago, when we started to raise the issues of preparation for retirement, of which financial and health planning issues are the major parts, we considered retirement as a continuous period from cessation of work to death. The problems of frailty and widowhood were less seriously considered. Now, I suspect that it may be wiser to plan for two phases of retirement: the first from sixty or sixty-five to about seventy-five, and the second from early frailty and diminished vigour to the end of the road. It may be that the last phase may not start until around eighty, but the second phase does pose different physical problems requiring different solutions.

Increasing longevity means that the family home, or the new retirement home, in this country or abroad, may be entirely suitable for the reasonably active but can impose severe burdens on anybody frail. I accept that it is easy to preach this but difficult to think about objectively, particularly as the older you get, the more you tend to fear change. Experience has taught, and again it is easier to preach than decide, that the trick is to move a little too early rather than when it is inevitable. Not only is it easier for an active person to be accepted into sheltered housing, but also their health and well-being are better for being supported. Single people, or those who become single by bereavement, be they men or women, have special problems in retirement planning because they do need the support of other people. There is a strong case, unless they 'have family', for them to move early, perhaps at retirement, into a supportive system which provides company and stimulation.

All this may sound gloomy but you must face the fact that between seventy-five and eighty you will, unless you are lucky enough to die suddenly, sooner or later require support. For the same reasons, there will be a time when there is only one of you who will be in a more critical situation and requiring more help. It is only sensible to think about this well in advance and plan a smooth progression. For the first time, couples are beginning to need extra care because they can no longer look after each other and the Abbeyfield Society is beginning to provide this, whereas most Part III long stay accommodation demands separation.

Against this background then, what are the options? These will obviously be determined by your financial resources, personal inclinations and family support. They will also be influenced by any decision you took when you first retired.

You need to do several bits of homework, whether you retire at home or abroad:

- Will your retirement home be suitable when you cannot manage stairs or get the shopping up the hill?
- Do you have reasonable faith in the local medical facilities, both in terms of the doctors and the hospitals? If not, what are you proposing to do?
- Will your money last out?
- Are there any sheltered housing units in the area with built-in medical support? If so, should you be on the waiting list and can you afford it?
- When there is only one of you, will he/she want to stay or come back to the UK? If so, where will they go?

If you retire abroad, it may well be sensible to consider making use of UK medical facilities, either private or NHS. To this end, it is vital to see that the right payments have been made and forms completed. I know that BUPA type insurance cover for older people is expensive but it may well be sensible to try to keep it up. At present, it is possible to maintain UK eligibility for a range of support under some circumstances, so check on this.

If you decide to stay in the UK, perhaps in the same house, the same questions have to be answered. For most readers, when they get to eighty, their original home may well be too big and unadaptable. Thus, at some stage, a smaller house, smaller garden or flat with a lift may be desirable.

Our basic thinking in the Pre-Retirement Association is perhaps a smaller house or bungalow in the same area where you are known, or near a key family member who will keep an eye on you. If there is good family support, it could be sensible to think ahead to a 'granny flat' or bungalow where one or both of you can be independent.

In theory, it should be possible under the NHS to get home help and nursing but availability varies as does the willingness of your doctor to fight for it. Given a choice too, it is wise to select an area with good medical resources and nursing homes. Home nursing is also privately available through agencies but twenty-four hour cover is expensive and only partially covered by insurance.

The next option, and probably the most difficult, is when the home/family situation becomes too difficult and you need to consider sheltered accommodation. This consideration falls into two broad categories: the public and the private, and between the two come the charitably run and voluntary housing associations which provide facilities in which you pay to live, as in fact you do in local authority sheltered housing. Again your options will be determined by your financial resources.

Local authority housing depends on residential eligibility and, of course, availability. But things are improving; units are getting smaller and new regulations are raising the standards of private accommodation. The present problem is shortage of capital from central and local government. Sooner or later, this will improve and more facilities become available. I say this because it has become the policy of government, based on the realisation that well-run voluntary organisations can give better value for money than bureaucratic local authority units.

This then leaves consideration of the currently popular commercially provided sheltered housing enclaves. These are still in an evolutionary phase but the numbers are increasing rapidly. In essence, you purchase a flat, maisonette or bungalow and pay a service charge. Not all of them are designed to cope with frailty. Such a unit may be a good and pleasant option and well worth considering even if it will not take you all the way down the road. Given a choice, go for the one with the most built-in medical back-up.

Because there are now so many of these, and more on the way, it is not practicable to give detailed descriptions but the addresses below will point you in the right direction. Look at service charges and what you get, resale possibilities and reversion options. Make sure that the character of the unit will be preserved with change of ownership and residents. In a commercial world, this needs safeguarding, very much as in blocks of flats.

This leaves us with the difficult problem of extra care, or support for those who cannot cope on their own. There are three main options:

(1) The local authority or NHS long stay hospital or Part III accommodation. The policy now is to get away from hospitals and move towards smaller 'homes' backed up by day centres and domiciliary support. The aim is to return people to the community and provide support from Social Service professionals and help for building alterations. In practice, this is patchy and limited but can be expected to improve.

If you do run out of money, local authorities have a responsibility to provide accommodation, so that if facilities are not available, Social Services can be persuaded to support residents in private or voluntary equivalent homes. It is a battle to get this and the possibilities vary with location and changing regulations.

(2) The voluntary Abbeyfield Society type organisation. These are non-profit-making bodies which are usually better at covering the spectrum of need. Because of my experience, I am biased in favour of the Abbeyfield approach. For the lonely single person, it blends independence and support. There are 900 houses all over the country and the growing availability of related 'extra care' houses.

The trick is to get in while you are still a goer and perhaps sniff them out by a week's visit without commitment. This can in fact be a better solution because by being near, but not on top of the family, you will be less of a burden.

Abbeyfield, particularly, provides a range of houses at different income levels and social classes.

(3)   The nursing home. These are mostly privately run and for profit and vary from the admirable to the awful and, in price, from fair and reasonable to exorbitant. Current fair prices for the better of these and extra care is from about £200 per week. The new 1984/5 regulations for inspection and regulation will certainly raise the standard of some and close others. The probability is that this sector will both grow and improve. They also vary in the degree of frailty or illness they can handle. The only answer is to shop around, have a look and take local advice. Local authorities and other organisations listed will give you addresses.

It is worth remembering that acute terminal or other serious illness is a lesser problem because the NHS hospital service still gives good cover for this and rehabilitation facilities are improving.

Long stay frailty which may be for two or more years is the difficulty and it seems to me that if the family cannot cope, the choice lies between the voluntary and the private nursing home. Your doctor should have a good overview of what is locally available and which are the best buys.

Essentially, the options you have depend on forward planning. This is both financial and domestic and the important point is not to leave the choice too late and be forced into a crisis option.

Sources of information

As has been said in the text the Sheltered Housing scene is one not only of change and evolution, but also varies across the country. Thus it is only sensible to list organisations and agencies which will supply the information about what is available in any specific area, or where to go for local details. On this basis help might be had from:

The Local Housing Authority, the Director of Social Services, Town Hall, Public Library and Citizens Advice Bureau

Age Concern England
Bernard Sunley House
60 Pitcairn Road
Mitcham
Surrey CR4 3LL

Counsel and Care for the Elderly
131 Middlesex Street
London E1
(Very good at advice on financial support and some nursing
homes)

National Federation of Housing Associations
175 Gray's Inn Road
London WC1X 8UP

The Abbeyfield Society
186 Darkes Lane
Potters Bar
Herts EN6 1AB

New Homes Marketing Board
82 New Cavendish Street
London W1M 8AD

Help The Aged
St James Walk
London EC1R 0BE

Part Two
Financial Aspects

7 Introduction

The most important aspect of financial planning is to identify your objectives at an early stage, consult relevant professional advisers, and direct your financial resources towards achieving the objectives that you have identified. There are really three different situations:

(1)   the person planning ahead for his retirement in the future;
(2)   a person about to retire in the immediate future who wishes to maximise his post retirement income;
(3)   a person (usually somewhat older) who wishes to take steps to reduce the capital transfer tax which will be payable on his eventual death (whilst still retaining his financial independence).

The following chapters will contain a great deal of information which is relevant to all three situations, but the purpose of this introduction is to draw out the wider considerations which need to be borne in mind at each stage (essentially it is a question of asking yourself the right questions).

Pre-retirement planning

A person aged fifty should look ahead, and relevant questions to ask yourself are as follows:

Will you receive the maximum pension permitted by the legislation? (see p 87)

- Have you moved jobs and do you have a frozen pension under your previous employers' scheme?
- Will your pension be restricted if you take early retirement?

● Could you buy back years or additional pension related to notional remuneration such as benefits in kind

If you are self-employed (see p 105)

● Have you paid the maximum allowable retirement annuity premiums?
● If you employ your wife could you provide her with pension benefits?

Capital gains tax planning (see p 97)

● Will you qualify for the £100,000 CGT relief on the sale of your business or family company on retirement?
● Can you take any action to enable your wife to qualify for the maximum relief as well as you?

Investment planning (see p 119)

● How can you best build up capital over the years running up to retirement?

Financial planning for those about to retire (see p 93)

It is of course absolutely essential to compare like with like. The true comparison is not between gross pay and gross pension, but rather between net pay and *net* pension. So don't be despondent, or worry unnecessarily. On the other hand, you should make allowance for inflation in your plans for the future.

Most of what is contained in the following chapters will concentrate on your problems, and the facts will probably speak for themselves provided that you ask the right questions. However, retirement can be a confusing time and the following quiz may help to focus your attention on the salient aspects.

● How much pension will you receive?
● What pension can you commute to a lump sum?
● Do you have to take a reduced pension in order to leave a pension for your wife?
● Have you any frozen pensions from any previous jobs?
● Have you a private pension? Has your wife?
● What is the value of your house?

● How many life policies do you have?
● What is their surrender value now? Their value at maturity?
● What other investments do you have:
    bank or building society deposits
    savings certificates
    share options
    shares
    gilts
    second home?
● Will you be liable to capital gains tax on the disposal of any investments?
● Can you expect any inheritance? Can your wife?
● Have you any investment income or consultancy earnings?
● Have you any hobby that could be income producing?
● Have you any mortgages or loans?
● At what date do they cease and is it tax efficient to clear them early?

It is also necessary to examine your future expenditure, the following are those types of expenditure which would normally arise:

Home insurance
Life insurance
Private health insurance
Rates (including water rates)
Mortgage or rent
Electricity
Gas
Oil
Decoration, repairs
Housekeeping and food
Household equipment
Furniture, carpets
Telephone
Garden
Clothes
Fares
Car tax
Car insurance
Car maintenance

AA/RAC subscription
Petrol, oil
Papers, periodicals, books
Hobbies
Club subscriptions
Theatre, cinema
Television, video
Holidays
Hairdresser
Cigarettes, tobacco, confectionery
Beverages
Charities, donations
Postage
Miscellaneous gifts, birthdays,
    Christmas etc
Chemist sundries
Prescriptions
Dentist
Optician

Another approach is to take a year's supply of your bank statements, cheque book stubs and statements from any credit card companies, to ensure as far as possible that you have listed *all* of your expenditure, noting any extraordinary items that do not occur on a regular basis.

Capital transfer tax planning (see p 149)

Most elderly people are reluctant to take action which will significantly reduce their spendable income or curtail their financial independence or flexibility. This is understandable. On the other hand, people in this position want to know about CTT to see whether there is relatively simple action which they could take which would help them to reduce the burden of this tax which will eventually fall upon their family. If ways can be put forward of saving on CTT without giving up income or flexibility these will generally be favourably received.

Having said this, the sooner you start to take steps to deal with your CTT problem (or rather your family's CTT problem) the more that can be achieved. Some of the possibilities are set out in the following chapters, but it is worth doing a quick 'totting-up' exercise now to see what CTT could be payable upon your eventual death:

Value

- How much is your house worth?
- Personal effects, car etc?
- Portfolio investments?
- Building society and bank deposits?
- Other land, shares in private companies?

_____

Deduct debts, mortgages etc

_____

=======

This will only be a rough indication, as there are special rules which may affect the position (for example, if you have made substantial lifetime gifts or are a beneficiary under a trust). However, the following rates apply on death and your family will probably have to pay far more than you would have thought prior to doing this exercise.

Amount of Transfer	Rate	Total Tax
£000s	%	£
0–67	Nil	Nil
67–89	30	6,600
89–122	35	18,150
122–155	40	31,350
155–194	45	48,900
194–243	50	73,400
243–299	55	104,200
Over 299	60	

8 Pre-retirement planning

It is generally accepted that it is necessary for everyone to make adequate financial provision for the day that they retire. Sound planning will then allow them to do the things that the commitments of a career have prevented, and travel, hobbies etc will be much more possible given the freedom that retirement provides.

Of course it will be necessary to have a healthy income if full advantage is to be taken of this new freedom, and nowadays most people plan well ahead to ensure that their retirement is not clouded by financial problems; in the certain knowledge that the state benefits to which they are entitled will hardly be adequate. This section deals with the main methods of retirement planning.

Pension schemes

Most people are aware that pension schemes offer one of the best means of saving for retirement. At present pension funds have three distinct advantages over other forms of saving:

(1) pension funds are exempt from all UK taxes, and accordingly the sum invested accumulates in value at a higher rate than other savings media;
(2) at retirement part of the pension may be commuted for a tax-free lump sum;
(3) pension contributions attract tax relief up to the highest rate of tax.

Given these tax advantages, it is obvious that everyone saving for retirement should make maximum use of the Inland Revenue allowances.

This appears now to be more important than a few years ago in view of the recent uncertainty that has arisen over the State Earnings Related Scheme (see p 100). It is now intended that this scheme will be phased out in the forthcoming Social Security review, and this will place an increased emphasis on personal pension arrangements, either through a company pension scheme or a personal pension scheme.

Topping up a company pension scheme

It is rare for a person to be entitled to as much from a pension scheme as the Inland Revenue would allow him to have. If your earnings exceed your need for income, it can be advantageous for you to save by making use of a scheme which permits people to pay money as additional voluntary contributions towards their pension. Many employers have these additional voluntary contribution (AVC) schemes, frequently linked to building society investment, while others are operated through insurance companies.

Everyone is free to contribute up to fifteen per cent of his income towards a pension scheme and can claim full tax relief on this. In practice few pension schemes require contributions on anything like this scale. The difference between the five or six per cent which may be contributed to the main pension scheme and the full fifteen per cent entitlement can be paid in AVC. Not only is full tax relief available on these amounts, but the funds accumulate free of UK tax until retirement. At that time they are treated in exactly the same way as any other pension entitlement.

A typical use of an AVC scheme would be when a person anticipates that he will not be able to afford to commute part of his pension from the main scheme for cash. He can use his AVCs to accumulate a cash sum and provided this falls within the allowances he can take the whole amount. This is far more effective than any other means of saving which is open to him. Until 1984, he could use life assurance and obtain partial tax relief on premiums. Here, however, he obtains full tax relief on them. In addition, the gross roll-up of the fund free from income and capital gains tax can produce a much better result.

Salary sacrifice

A salary sacrifice arrangement is one where a person gives up some of his salary, with the amount that he has given up being paid into an approved pension scheme. Income tax relief is obtained at the individual's top rate because the amount given up no longer forms part of his taxable income. Salary sacrifice arrangements are especially attractive for the high income earner. There can also be a useful saving in the employer's National Insurance contributions, so the company saves 10.45 per cent of the amount given up by the employee.

A salary sacrifice requires the agreement of both the company and the employee and must be properly documented in order to obtain Inland Revenue approval. Provided it does so, the advantages are considerable, especially where the individual has considerably underfunded his pension provision.

Personal pension schemes

If you do not belong to a company pension scheme or if you are self-employed then you may arrange a personal pension scheme. Like a company scheme member, the amount you may contribute is laid down by the Inland Revenue and at the present time the limits are as follows:

$$
\begin{array}{ll}
\text{Born in 1934 onwards} & 17\tfrac{1}{2}\% \\
1916 \text{ to } 1933 & 20\% \\
1914 \text{ to } 1915 & 21\% \\
1912 \text{ to } 1913 & 24\% \\
1910 \text{ to } 1911 & 26\tfrac{1}{2}\%
\end{array}
$$

These percentages apply to 'net relevant earnings' which can be broadly defined as earnings from your non-pensionable employment or business, less certain deductions such as expenses, trading losses, capital allowances etc.

If you are in a position of having two sources of income, one from pensionable employment and the other being net relevant earnings, you may contribute up to the above limit in respect of your net relevant earnings regardless of the level of your pensionable earnings.

In addition to the above limits, you are also allowed to make a contribution in respect of unpaid contributions during the previous six years. Thus for those making their first retirement contribution in the 1985/86 tax year, an additional sum may also be paid in respect of 1979/80 and subsequent years. As a means of providing for retirement this is an especially useful allowance.

In the introduction it was stated that it is sensible to plan well ahead. This principle applies especially to pension schemes as the following table (which is based upon typical assumptions on investment return) illustrates.

Annual pension contribution £1,000.00 (£700 net of relief at 30%)	
Age next birthday	Estimated pension fund at age 60
	£
35	148,000
40	80,000
45	42,000
50	20,000

('Projections' given by various insurance companies will vary according to projected bonus rates, assumptions regarding unit growth etc but to some extent the precise assumptions used in this projection do not matter: any insurance company, actuary or other qualified adviser will strongly recommend that you start a pension plan as soon as you can afford to do so.)

As the figures show, a delay of five years in starting a pension is expensive and may also cause a considerable financial burden in later years as an effort is made to make up for the lost time.

Frozen pensions

Employees who have changed jobs in their working lives may well be entitled to a pension in respect of their previous employment. Section 32 of the Finance Act 1981 now enables insurance companies to offer an alternative to a frozen pension in the form of a 'buy out' bond, or 'Section 32 scheme' plan as they are commonly known.

On changing jobs, an ex-employee can now arrange to invest the transfer value of the pension into an insurance company annuity, provided the agreement of the scheme trustees is obtained. These bonds often offer the chance of a higher pension in retirement and those who have a frozen pension would be advised to investigate the possibilities for themselves.

A pension for your wife

Many men who are in business or a profession employ their wives, mainly on a part-time basis where the salary is insufficient to attract income tax and National Insurance contributions. Where the husband's income is taxed under Schedule D, it is possible to arrange a pension scheme for the wife as an employee, and obtain tax relief on the pension contributions as an expense to the business.

Given the relatively low salary involved, you may think that such an arrangement would not be worthwhile. This is almost certainly not so. As we explain in a later chapter, the maximum pension which an employee can receive at retirement is two-thirds of salary at that time. In order to ensure that people are not unduly restricted in terms of their pension contributions, the Inland Revenue will allow the employee's present day salary to be escalated by 8.5 per cent per year to their normal retirement date, and approve contributions that will fund a pension of two-thirds of this sum. Thus, it is possible for worthwhile contributions to be made even though the current salary appears not to justify them.

This is particularly attractive to those who pay tax at the higher rates during their working lives, but find that their tax rate falls on retirement. A pension for your wife can shelter savings from the effects of higher rate tax, and repay them with interest when your tax liabilities have reduced.

Tax shelters

A further way of supplementing your retirement income is to save regularly from income to produce a lump sum at age sixty or sixty-five. There are numerous schemes for just this purpose but some are not particularly tax efficient where the higher rate taxpayer is concerned. In this case the need is for a scheme that will shelter the profit on the savings from the ravages of tax and there is no better arrangement than an insurance company maximum investment plan. By investing via a life assurance company the capital growth and income are taxed at the rates applicable to insurance companies, and not those which apply to individuals. Thus a savings scheme of this type is still attractive in certain situations despite the abolition of life premium tax relief in 1984.

Where some will wish to create a capital sum for retirement, others may have capital which they similarly wish to invest in a tax efficient way. In these cases investment bonds issued by insurance companies may be attractive as the appreciation within the bond is not taxed until such time as the investment is cashed in and then is liable only to tax at the higher rates. Thus, investment bonds with their ability to defer a tax charge can shelter investment income until after retirement when the investor's tax rate will often fall to the basic rate and the bond can be redeemed without a tax liability.

Another way of deferring taxable income is to invest in an offshore 'roll-up' fund. These are companies based offshore in the Isle of Man and Channel Islands and operated by leading UK financial institutions. The underlying investments are in bank deposits and very short-term fixed-interest investments. Income from these investments is not distributed as dividends but accumulated, or 'rolled-up'. The companies operate in a similar way to unit trusts so that the investor realises the benefit of the accumulated income when he sells his shares. The profit is subject to income tax, but the investor can effectively choose the year in which he has taxable income — and in the meantime his money is accumulating interest without any tax whatsoever!

There are many other lump sum investment vehicles that are available which also enjoy favourable tax treatment. National Savings Certificates are a good example and the prudent investor will spread his capital across a number of assets to achieve the best results from the tax standpoint. Our section on fixed interest and capital growth investments explains each of these schemes in detail.

9 Financial planning for those about to retire

So far we have concentrated on long-term planning for retirement, we turn now to the problems (and planning opportunities!) of those who are much closer to retirement.

Choosing the right retirement date

It can make quite a lot of difference whether one retires at the beginning or the end of a Tax Year. One situation where timing can be crucial is where a person receives a golden handshake on retirement. To understand this it is necesary to go into some detail on the way in which golden handshakes and compensation payments are taxed.

Golden handshakes and compensation payments are known to the Inland Revenue as 'termination payments'. They are treated as income which arises at the date the employment terminates. It therefore makes no difference that the actual payment may be delayed until the next tax year; if A's employment ceased on the 31 March 1985, his golden handshake is assessed for 1984/85 even though it may be paid on 6 April 1985 or later during the tax year 1985/86.

A golden handshake is taxable in full as income if the director/employee is entitled to it under his contract of employment. In other cases there is an exemption for the first £25,000. This exemption applies whether the payment is expressed to be ex-gratia or a compensation payment.

For the sake of completeness, it should also be mentioned that statutory redundancy payments are not themselves taxable, but they do consume part of the £25,000 exemption.

Example 1

B receives compensation of £20,000 and statutory redundancy payments of £8,000. The redundancy payments are exempt, but mean that part of the compensation is taxable:

Compensation		£20,000
Exemption	£25,000	
Less	8,000	17,000
Taxable amount		£3,000

Top-slicing relief

A further relief is given in the form of a reduction in the rate of tax. The tax charged on the first £25,000 chargeable (ie after deducting the exemption) is at fifty per cent of the rate which would otherwise be payable and the next £25,000 is charged at seventy-five per cent of the normal rate.

Example 2

If C receives a golden handshake of £40,000 and had other taxable income in that year of £28,000 the tax payable on the £15,000 which is taxable would be computed as follows:

Total taxable income	£43,000	tax thereon	£18,375.00
Deduct tax payable on other income	£28,000		£10,200.00
			£ 8,175.00
Tax actually payable on the £40,000 compensation is 50% of £8,175.00 ie			£ 4,087.50

Timing of retirement

It should now be obvious that the best time to terminate an employment is at the very start of a tax year if your marginal rate of tax will be lower after retirement. The effect of the top-slicing relief will often be to eliminate tax entirely if you retire on 6 April.

There is also a planning point for the self-employed. Your retirement may give rise to a cessation for Schedule D purposes (see *Allied Dunbar Tax Guide*) and this means that the Inland Revenue may be able to increase your tax assessments for the two years preceding the year of your retirement. In some cases it may be worth deferring your retirement until shortly after 5 April, so as to limit the extent of the Inland Revenue's adjustments for past years.

The Revenue's powers arise from the fact that self-employed earnings are assessed on the preceding year basis. The Revenue are permitted to tax your actual earnings for the year of cessation and to adjust the assessments for the 'penultimate' years if this results in an overall increase (the Revenue cannot just adjust one year in isolation).

Example 3

A is self-employed and has an accounting date of 30 June. His profits and tax assessments have been as follows:

		Assessed tax year
Year ended 30 June 1982	£15,000	1983/84
Year ended 30 June 1983	£20,000	1984/85
Year ended 30 June 1984	£25,000	1985/86

If A retires on 5 April 1986 and his last two years' results were £30,000 (year ended 30 June 1985) and £15,000 (nine month period ended 5 April 1986) the Revenue would replace the 1985/86 assessment with the actual earnings for the year of £22,500 (ie 3×12 profits for the year to 30 June 1985 + the profits for the final nine months) and the two preceding years would be adjusted as follows:

1983/84:	3/12 × profits for year ended 30 June 1983	5,000
	9/12 × profits for year ended 30 June 1984	18,750
		£23,750

1984/85:	3/12 × profits for year ended 30 June 1984	6,250
	9/12 × profits for year ended 30 June 1985	22,500
		£28,750

Thus additional income would be assessed for 1983/84 of £8,750 and a similar adjustment made for 1984/85.

If A delayed his retirement until 6 April 1986, the Revenue could not adjust 1983/84 and the adjustments for the two following years would not be so great in total.

It is important to take professional advice on such a matter as the timing of a cessation. Special provisions may apply where a person has been a member of a Partnership.

Last minute pension contributions

When a person draws near to his retirement date it is worth considering whether additional voluntary contributions or self-employed pension contributions can be paid. Even though the money may be with the insurance company for a relatively short time, the fact that the contributions attract income tax relief and a lump sum may be taken tax-free mean that there is often substantial advantage in paying such contributions.

Example 4

A woman approaching sixty decides to pay a retirement annuity contribution. A single payment of £1,000 would attract thirty per cent income tax relief and so the net cost would be only £700. If she took the benefits from age sixty-one she might expect to receive a tax-free lump sum of £330 plus an on-going pension of £101. Effectively the pension represents a return on an overall outlay of £370, ie:

Premium Paid	£1,000
less tax relief	300
	700
less tax free lump sum	330
	£370

The benefits can be even greater for a person who is subject to tax at the maximum rate of sixty per cent.

Example 5

A man aged sixty-four is due to retire on his sixty-fifth birthday in three months' time. If he pays £5,000 retirement annuity premiums the following position is likely to obtain:

Retirement annuity premium	£5,000
less tax relief	£3,000
	£2,000
less tax free lump sum	£1,370
Net cost	£ 630

In return for this net outlay, he could expect to receive an on-going pension of £380 per annum.

Don't forget that you can pay retirement annuity premiums if you have non-pensionable earnings even though you may also have pensionable earnings from another employment.

Capital gains tax on the sale of your business/private company

This is another area where the timing of your retirement may be very important. Even if you cannot avoid payment of CGT, it would obviously be more beneficial to dispose of your business/company on 6 April rather than 5 April. The additional delay in the payment of CGT for twelve months can be very valuable in these times of high interest rates. It may, on the other hand, be possible to reduce the liability if the gain can be deferred until such time as you are entitled to the full CGT retirement relief.

This relief is available in the following circumstances:

(1)   the person realising the gain must be at least 60 (or must be being forced to retire because of ill-health);
(2)   the person must have been engaged in the trade or have been a full-time working director of a family trading company;
(3)   the gain must arise on the sale of the business or shares

in the family company or of an asset owned by the person but used rent free by the business or company.

The maximum relief is available only if the person has carried on business or been a full-time working director for the ten years preceding the disposal.

Both husband and wife can qualify for the full £100,000 relief if they meet the necessary conditions (for further detail on this see *Allied Dunbar Tax Guide*).

The way in which the relief operates can be complex and professional advice should be taken, but in principle you should time a disposal on retirement so as to ensure that full advantage is taken of the relief. All other things being equal it may pay to carry on another year rather than retire at (say) age fifty-nine and pay substantial amounts of capital gains tax.

Checklist for year of retirement

- Will it be beneficial to defer the date of your retirement because you will receive a golden handshake?
- If you are self-employed, can you mitigate the tax consequences of a cessation of business on your retirement?
- Can you pay further retirement annuity premiums?
- Take advice on the sale of your private business or family company so as to minimise any capital gains tax.
- Employees with share options (see *Allied Dunbar Tax Guide*) should take professional advice to ensure that any income tax charge on the exercise of the options is kept as low as possible.

10 Your pension and what to do with it

Most people when they retire become entitled to a number of different pensions. To begin with there is the basic state retirement pension, in addition to which there may well be benefits from the state earnings related scheme. On top of these, it is likely in many cases that the individual will also be entitled to a pension from his employer's pension scheme, or to a private pension (or 'retirement annuity') in the case of those who were either in non-pensionable employment or who were self-employed.

State pensions

The starting point for anyone concerned about their income in retirement must be to establish exactly what pension can be expected from the state. There is some confusion in the minds of many people about this subject because of all the changes that have taken place in the past. In 1978 a completely new pension scheme (SERPS) was introduced which has yet to take full effect and which may soon be dismantled or reduced. However, for those people retiring today there is a useful pension from this source.

At present the state retirement pension can be divided into its two parts:

The basic flat rate retirement pension

This is currently £1,861.60 per annum for a single person and £2,979.60 per annum for a married couple. This is raised by the government in line with the Retail Price Index in November of each year.

To qualify for the full pension you must have paid sufficient National Insurance contributions during your working life; and this is defined as paying contributions for about ninety per cent of your working life between the ages of sixteen and sixty-five (or sixty for women). For those who have not satisfied these conditions, then a reduced pension will be paid. You should receive a pension claim form from the Department of Health and Social Security about four months before you retire and if you do not receive this, then you should make enquiries at your local DHSS office.

If you are a married woman and your husband is still working, a pension can still be claimed at the rate applicable to the single person provided you are age sixty and you have paid enough National Insurance contributions in your own right. Alternatively, you can claim a pension based on your husband's contributions when he retires. A degree of care must be exercised in this regard, as there are a number of options available and the choice of pension will depend on individual circumstances.

The earnings related scheme

In addition to the basic flat rate pension, you may be entitled to additional benefits from the state earnings related scheme, although many people are contracted out of it. As its name suggests, benefits under this scheme are related to your salary. If you are contracted into the scheme you will build up a pension at the rate of $1\frac{1}{4}$ per cent of your earnings between the lower and upper limits was for each year of contribution since April 1978 (subject to a maximum of twenty years).

In 1984/85 the lower earnings limit was £147.33 per month and the upper limit was £1,083.33. Each year's earnings are revalued annually until normal retirement in line with movements in national average earnings. In consequence, a person retiring in April 1985 who has contributed at the maximum rate throughout the scheme will be entitled to receive an additional pension of approximately £1,000 per annum. Thereafter the pension, like the flat rate pension, is linked to the retail price index.

A widow may inherit the whole of her husband's earnings related pension and will become entitled to the basic flat rate pension at the single person's rate.

Before the state earnings related scheme was introduced, there was another scheme in force known as the state graduated pension scheme. You may be entitled to some benefits from this in addition to the state earnings related pension, but the extra amount is not significant.

All these pensions are of particular importance because they are linked to the cost of living and will retain their value. The flat rate pension makes a significant contribution to either a single person's or a married couple's budget and the state earnings related pension already provides a considerable addition to this. In a few more years it will be much more important.

Private pensions

Most people who work for companies belong to occupational pension schemes as well as the state ones. Some of these are contracted out of the state earnings related pension, whereas others operate on top of it. If you are contracted out you will not receive an earnings related pension but your private pension must be at least equal to the state pension and will almost certainly produce better benefits. In most cases, a private scheme will provide a pension which is vastly better than that available from the state.

The actual conditions of pension schemes vary from one company to another but the best provision which can be made is determined by the Inland Revenue. Generally, the maximum pension which an employee can receive at normal retirement date is two-thirds of his salary at that time. In practice many schemes provide a pension of one-sixtieth of final salary for each year of service. This produces a maximum pension entitlement of two-thirds after a person has been working with the company for forty years. It is, however, increasingly common for additional benefits to be given to senior staff who have joined late in their career.

The definition of final salary is often complex in order to protect a person whose earnings fall in the last year of his working life. If you are concerned to compare the details of the scheme to which you belong with others, there is an excellent *Allied*

Hambro Pensions Guide by Tony Reardon (Longman Professional) which covers the subject.

However, the problem facing most people in retirement is simply to establish what benefits they will get under their scheme and this can best be done by consulting your employer.

Choosing a pension

The beneficiaries of pension schemes are usually given a choice of how they wish the income to be paid. It is possible to have an annuity which will only continue for as long as one person survives. Alternatively, you can get a smaller annuity which will continue throughout the life of both husband and wife. The size of the reduction depends upon their ages. If they are both sixty-five, a fund of £10,000 would provide them with a lifetime income of, for example, £1,275 per annum. Under similar conditions a single man of sixty-five would have got £1,550.

The choice of the appropriate type of pension depends upon your circumstances. A popular choice for married couples is a pension which continues at a lower rate after the first death. This protects the survivor but recognises the fact that one can live more cheaply than two.

Commutation

It is normal for a person at retirement to be given the option of commuting a part of his pension for a tax-free lump sum. This is a valuable benefit but many people are not sure whether it is really to their advantage to cash in their pension and have difficulty making up their minds whether or not to take advantage of the opportunity.

At first sight, the choice between a tax-free sum now and taxable pension seems straightforward. Even if you do not need the money now, it seems more sensible to take it. This may, however, be an over-simplification and some people may be better off with the pension.

The Inland Revenue restricts the size of the tax-free lump sum which can be given. The maximum allowed is one and a half times a person's final remuneration (including benefits in kind), but smaller amounts must be given to those with less than twenty years' service. The most critical question is how much pension must be sacrificed in return for the lump sum. There is a table of factors which has been agreed among the insurance companies and the actuaries who run independent pension schemes:

	Age	*Factor*
Men	60	10.2
	65	9.0
	70	7.8
Women	55	12.2
	60	11.0
	65	9.8

The factors for other ages can be calculated by an increase or decrease of 0.02 per month of age. In order to calculate the reduction in pension, the lump sum should be divided by it. Thus, a woman retiring at sixty and receiving a tax-free lump sum of £11,000 would have her pension reduced by £1,000 per annum.

A pension scheme does not have to use these factors and can choose others which are less favourable. Let us, however, look at the position of a man of sixty-five who commutes £2,000 worth of pension for a cash sum of £18,000. He can invest this money in a purchased life annuity from a life company. This will give him a gross income of £2,800 at current rates. £1,260 of it will be tax-free, leaving only £1,540 taxable. This gives a net income after basic rate tax of £2,338 in contrast to £1,400 from the pension. By taking the cash sum and reinvesting it, the net income after tax has increased by £938.

This is a perfectly valid comparison if the pension in the scheme is properly comparable to the annuity which has been bought from the insurance company. There will probably be one or two minor differences since pensions are normally paid monthly, whereas purchased life annuities are usually payable half yearly. These are, however, of little significance. What matters is that a great many superannuation schemes will increase pensions in course of payment. Insurance companies do not do this for annuities unless it is part of the contract.

This makes it difficult to compare the pension which has to be surrendered with the value of the cash sum. If inflation revives and your pension scheme increases the benefit in payment to match it, the income payable will soon overtake any annuity which can be purchased for the cash sum. On the other hand, inflation may decline and even if it does not, your pension scheme may not keep pace with it.

Pensions in the public sector normally match inflation, but almost no private ones do this. However, a high proportion of the major employers in the private sector make discretionary increase to pensions in payment and in recent years these have tended to match inflation.

The best way of assessing your position is to find out the record of your employer over the last few years. If there is no contractual obligation on him to continue making increase, there is a strong moral one. If pensions have kept pace with the cost of living in the past then it is likely that they will do so in the future. If they have not done so, then you should not expect them to in the future unless you have clear evidence of a change of heart. In the absence of any increase it is clearly to your advantage to take the cash sum. If on the other hand you can expect a pension which will more or less keep pace with inflation the decision is much more finely balanced. On pure investment grounds you are probably better off to stick with the highest possible pension, although this could be a mistake if inflation continues to reduce.

Of course, investment considerations are not the only ones. If the pension you will receive is more than sufficient after commuting a portion and you have uses for the cash you should of course take it. The fact remains that many people find that as retirement approaches they have more than sufficient cash and when this is the case they can simply choose the most commercially advantageous arrangement.

There are a few pension schemes in which the pension increases automatically after retirement. When this is the case, the commutation value of the pension will be different. In effect you will get more cash for each pound of pension sur-rendered.

Self-employed schemes

Where you have paid retirement annuity premiums, ie you have contributed to a personal pension scheme unconnected to an employer, then commutation is a reasonably straightfor-ward matter. Current legislation allows the insurance company to pay a tax-free lump sum which of course requires the sur-render of part of the pension entitlement. However, in most cases it is advantageous to take the cash and reinvest in a pur-chased life annuity, as this has a tax-free element (the 'capital content') which is not liable to income tax. This feature, there-fore, restricts the tax charge to only the interest element of the annuity and accordingly the after tax income is higher than it would be from the pension which is wholly taxable.

Open market options

Finally, when everything else has been done, it is important to ensure that you will obtain the maximum benefit from your pri-vate pension plan.

Most companies these days include in their contract an open market option. This enables a person to 'shop around' at the time of his retirement and use the funds which he has accumu-lated with one insurance company to buy an annuity from another if their rates are better. In practice, there is quite con-siderable variation on annuity rates and it is well worth looking around to ensure that the annuity quoted to you by your own insurance company is the best rate available.

As an indication of the amount of variation, the rates quoted in *Planned Savings* (at the time of writing) for a single life annuity for a man aged sixty-five and a fund of £10,000 varied from £1,477 to £1,530 per annum.

It should be noted that some insurance companies impose a 'transfer fee' or charge where a fund is transferred to another insurance company. Other companies give a 'loyalty bonus', ie the normal annuity rates are enhanced for people who have had a pension contract with the company concerned. Even so, it is still well worth obtaining competitive quotations.

11 Work after retirement

Working on a part-time basis

Many people are reluctant to give up work completely and choose to continue on a part-time basis. A number of considerations are relevant here:

Postponing your pension

It may be that if you are working, say, three days a week that you can afford to defer drawing your pension. This may enable the pension to be increased substantially when you eventually start to take it.

Paying into a private pension plan

If you do decide to draw your company pension and work part-time, don't forget that your part-time earnings will be non-pensionable earnings. Accordingly, you could obtain tax relief for retirement annuity premiums.

Example 6

A seventy-one year old man with part-time earnings of £5,000 could obtain tax relief for retirement annuity premiums of £1,000. The SPC contract might provide for a lump sum and annuity to be taken from age seventy-three. Assuming a marginal rate of tax of fifty-five per cent the figures might work out like this:

Retirement annuity premium	£1,000
less tax relief	550
net cost	450
less tax free lump sum	389
	61

Thus this exercise would result in an on-going pension of £106 per annum — leaving the individual in a profit position after only one year.

National Insurance aspects

Working after age sixty-five will not result in a restriction of the state pension unless you earn more than £70 per week.

National Insurance Contributions will not be payable by you after retirement but your employer may still be liable for contributions.

Working on a freelance basis

You will need to take professional advice which relates to your specific circumstances if you are going to have significant freelance earnings. However, the following are general considerations which should be borne in mind:

Preceding year basis of assesssment

The normal basis for assessment for a self-employed person is that his earnings for a tax year are taken to be the profits of his accounts which end in the preceding tax year.

Example 7

A draws up his accounts to 30 June. His profits for the year ended 30 June 1985 will determine the tax assessment for 1986/87. A special rule applies when a person starts a new business. His profits for the first tax year are based upon his actual earnings, and for the second tax year he is assessed on his earnings for the first twelve months of trading.

Example 8

A starts a business on 1 January 1985.

His results are as follows:

Year ended 31 December 1985	£ 6,000
Year ended 31 December 1986	£12,000
Year ended 31 December 1987	£15,000

The tax assessments would be:

1984/85 3/12 × £6,000	£ 1,500
1985/86 first 12 months	£ 6,000
1986/87 preceding year basis	£ 6,000

The basis of assessment suits A here as he is assessed on a total of £13,500 whereas his actual earnings for the period amounted to £33,000! However, if it had been the other way round, A could elect for his tax assesssments for his second and third year to be based on his actual profits. Note that the election can only be made by the taxpayer and that it cannot be made for one year in isolation.

In some cases it may be worth starting up in business with your wife as an employee and bringing her into partnership after the first twelve months. Another idea is to draw up accounts to 30 April so as to take full advantage of the preceding year basis (this assumes that profits will be increasing year by year). These are things which you should discuss with an accountant, together with matters such as:

● Can you claim expenses for using your home for business purposes?
● What other expenses will be allowable?
● Will you need to register for VAT purposes?

Working out your tax liability

As we have pointed out in Chapter 7, your gross income may go down after retirement but the reduction in your net spendable income may be less significant. You will no longer have certain expenses (eg your annual season ticket to get to work) and your investment income may increase — so there is no need to be despondent. Obviously, however, you need to do your sums and part of this budgeting process is to estimate your likely tax liability.

We have set out the stages in the computation in the form of a chart (see below). There should be sufficient information for most people but in cases of unusual complexity it may be necessary to refer to the *Allied Dunbar Tax Guide* (ie if you have foreign domicile, or are a Lloyd's Underwriter or own a farm etc). You may also need to take specialist advice if you cash in an insurance bond during the year (top-slicing relief will then usually be available but the computations are much too complex to go into here).

Working out your tax liability

(1) *Compute earned income*		Self	Wife	Tax paid
National Insurance pension			(i)	
Occupational pension				
Retirement annuity				
Income from employment				
Freelance earnings	(ii)			

Deduct retirement annuity relief
(see p 96)

                A

(2) *Compute investment income*		Self	Wife	Tax paid
National Savings Bank interest	(iii)			
Income from abroad	(iv)			
Income from property	(v)			
Dividends and taxed interest				
UK Bank and building society interest	(vi)			
	B			

(3) *Compute charges*		Self	Wife
Qualifying interest paid gross	(vii)		
Interest paid subject to MIRAS	(viii)		
Amount paid under charitable deeds of covenant	(ix)		
	C		

(4) *Compute other deductions*			
Business expansion scheme relief	(x)		
Allowable trading losses	(xi)		
	D		

                                     Totals for self and wife

Total income. (E)	A
	B
	C

Deduct   D   _____

                                                   _____

(5) *Compute personal allowances*   Self   Wife
     Single person's allowance   (xii)
     Married person's allowance   (xii)
     Wife's earned income allowance (xiv)

                                          F   _____ _____

                                               ════════ ════════

(6) *Tax liability*
Basically one deducts F from E and applies the following tables.
However note position on items in E which qualify only for higher rate
relief.

0–£16,200	30%
16,201–19,200	40%
19,201–24,400	45%
24,401–32,300	50%
32,301–40,200	55%
over 40,200	60%

Notes:
(i)   Is this amount paid by virtue of the wife's own contributions? If so
       wife's earned income allowance is due.
(ii)   This income will normally be assessable on the preceding year
       basis.
(iii) There is an exemption for the first £70 interest credited each year
       on the NSB ordinary account.
(iv)   This income will normally be assessable on the preceding year
       basis.
(v)   Does this include profits from furnished holiday accommodation?
       If so this counts as earned income.
(vi)   The next amount received should be grossed up, ie net building
       society interest of £100 is grossed income of £142.86 (£100 × $\frac{10}{7}$).
       Enter grossed-up figure in B and tax figure (ie $\frac{3}{7}$) in tax paid
       column.
(vii) This interest can be deducted from your taxable income for all tax
       purposes.
(viii) Interest paid under MIRAS does not qualify for basic rate relief
       but should be taken into account if you are subject to higher rate
       tax.
(ix)   The deed must require payments for a period of at least four
       years. A maximum of £10,000 qualifies for relief. Basic rate is
       deducted at source so these payments are relevant only if you are
       subject to higher rate tax.
(x) and (xi) See *Allied Dunbar Tax Guide.*
(xii) Basic allowance is £2,205. Age Allowance can increase this to
       £2,690 if income does not exceed £8,800.

(xiii)   Basic allowance is £3,455. Age Allowance can increase this to £4,255.
Marginal Age Allowance can be claimed, the excess of taxable income over £8,800 results in a reduction of the allowance of £2 for every £3 excess income.

(xiv)   Maximum relief is £2,205. The relief is limited to the amount of the wife's income if this is less.

Putting your savings to good use

Even if you have the maximum pension, there will still be a reduction in your income — at the very time that you have more opportunity to enjoy material comforts. Furthermore, the gap between your pension and your income requirements is likely to grow because of inflation. This is where your savings come in: invested judiciously they will produce income to augment your pension and to maintain your real income as you grow older.

Investment priorities

There is a vast range of different kinds of investment from which to choose. Each has its own particular advantages and drawbacks. You want to choose those which can give you the greatest number of important advantages while incurring the fewest significant disadvantages. After all, you have worked hard for your savings, now you want them to work for you.

The choice of investment depends both on your circumstances and your temperament, so that an investment which is attractive for one person may be quite unsuitable for another. Clearly, age has a great deal to do with an investor's 'perspective': as you get older income become more important than capital growth, guaranteed return and the ability to realise investments become more desirable, and so on. However, you must not lose sight of the need for capital growth, especially when you first retire. At the age of sixty, it is necessary to plan on the assumption that you or your wife (or both!) will survive to your eighties, and we all know how inflation can defeat the most sensible housekeeping over twenty years. You must protect the real value of your capital by investing at least part of it in a way that will produce capital growth in the longer term.

Cash flow is also very important and we must not lose sight of this. A very simple illustration of this is the choice which you get from a bank. It is no good putting money into a deposit account subject to one month's notice if you want to use it to pay bills this week. On the other hand, most current accounts do not pay you interest. What you need is sufficient in your current account to cover day to day needs, while any surplus is kept on deposit. In this way you get the best of both worlds. Indeed, some financial institutions have recognised this and introduced high interest bank accounts which are becoming more and more popular. These are effectively interest bearing current accounts with the full range of cheque book and other typical banking facilities. Some also have built in credit card and temporary loan facilities.

There are more than thirty different kinds of investment commonly used by ordinary people. Some of the categories contain hundreds or even thousands of different choices. There are now more than 700 unit trusts being actively promoted, and several new ones are started almost every week. Even more confusingly, there are more than a hundred life assurance companies, and each one of them offers a number of different policies. However, most investments can be divided into capital growth investments (shares, unit trusts, property, etc,) and fixed interest investments.

Striking a balance

Choosing an investment is not simply a matter of deciding how you can make the most of your money. It is not even a matter of choosing the investment that will produce the most money when you need it. In 1984 the Ordinary Share index on the London Stock Market moved up by some twenty-five per cent. This was obviously pleasing to most investors. The fact remains that the progress was not even. It rose sharply for the first four months of the year, and showed a gain of more than fifteen per cent. In the next two and a half months, it fell back to below the level at which it started the year. Thereafter it climbed back, and by October had regained its level of the early spring.

Clearly the fall in the late spring and early summer was of no significance if investors did not wish to sell their shares. You must really accept that part of the price of obtaining long-term capital growth is that you must expect these fluctuations. Fortunately, the income from shares and unit trusts does not fluctuate to the same extent and indeed should gradually rise, if the past is any guide to the future.

The fact remains that many people find these fluctuations worrying. If you can take the longer view, you should certainly consider equities (ie ordinary shares) and investment in unit trusts. If you are conservative, the extra return you may achieve will be spoiled by the worry that these fluctuations can cause, and you will be much better off if you invest most of your capital in fixed interest securities and other relatively safe investments. Even if you ignore the worry which fluctuating investments can cause, there is always the danger that a worried investor will liquidate his investment at the worst time. It is important to remember that for every person who buys shares at the bottom of the market, there is somebody else who sells them. As in most things, it is a question of striking the right balance. Only you can decide whether you wish to hold equities and capital growth investments. Normally they will produce better returns than fixed interest investments, *if* you can give them time to perform. However, even if you are psychologically prepared for the fluctuations in capital values, you may not be in a financial position to accept the attendant risks. It does not matter if you purchase such investments, provided you can choose the time when you sell them. The danger is that you may be forced to sell out when the market is depressed. You would be most unwise, therefore, to invest all of your capital in this way.

Whatever your attitude to taking risks, the first step in planning your investments is to assess your financial position. There is no point in choosing long-term investments if you will need cash in the short term (or may do so in an emergency). On the other hand, you do not want to keep money available if you do not need it, since you can usually obtain a higher return by investing on a longer-term basis.

We will come back to this subject of investment strategy later, but for now we will look at investments in a descriptive rather than a prescriptive way.

Analysis

There are a number of ways of looking at investments. Some of them are helpful, whereas others tell you more about the person who uses them than the investment itself. One of the most valuable ones grades them according to the degree of risk involved. At one end of the spectrum lies cash, which in theory carries no risk, but which of course also offers no chance of capital appreciation. At the other extreme are such things as commodity futures, or a bet on an outsider in the 3.30. Here the chances are that you will lose your money, but if you win, the benefit will be very great indeed. In theory at least, it is possible to give a position on this scale to every type of investment.

Another way of grading investments is according to their liquidity. This simply means how quickly an investment can be turned into cash. Money in your pocket or a current account at a bank can be put at one end of the scale. At the other end of the scale are investments like property which can take time to sell. The assesssment of liquidity is complicated by the fact that many illiquid investments can be used as security for a loan.

Traditionally these two measures were all that investors needed. The more risky or illiquid an investment was thought to be, the higher the potential return it offered. Sometimes the market would overestimate the risk attached to an investment which made it possible to obtain a relatively high return with comparatively little risk. Investment is primarily a matter of determining what risks you are able to run and how much liquidity you need.

These measures are valid today, but their assessment is greatly complicated by two factors. These are tax and inflation, both of which became increasingly important as the twentieth century went by. The last few years have seen both of them become less significant but it remains to be seen whether the change is permanent. Even if it is, both price rises and taxation remain much higher than they were twenty or twenty-five years ago.

Tax

Investments are taxed in different ways, depending upon their nature. The higher your tax rate, the more important this is. An investment which is appropriate for a person paying little tax may be unattractive to someone who pays tax at the higher rates.

Let us look at building society investment. At the time of writing, a 90 day investment share pays ten per cent with basic rate tax paid. This to the ordinary man is significantly better than the 12.25 per cent gross which is payable on a National Savings investment account. After allowing for tax at thirty per cent, the return on the National Savings investment is only 8.58 per cent. In contrast, however, a man who pays no tax at all would have done much better with the investment account, since he cannot reclaim the tax which the building society has paid. At the other extreme is the six per cent tax free which is paid on ordinary accounts of over £500 with the National Savings Bank up to a total interest of £70 per annum. This is not attractive to the man who pays no tax, and is outbid by the building society for the basic rate taxpayer. On the other hand, the man who pays tax at sixty per cent on any additional income will find the six per cent better than the 5.7 per cent which he will get after paying tax on the grossed up interest from the building society.

There is a simple rule for dealing with tax — always work out what the net return will be for you after tax. This is all that matters. Advertisements often like to quote gross yields. This is understandable,since the figures are much larger. Unfortunately, most of us will only receive our income after paying tax on it.

The taxation of capital gains, however, is much simpler. Everyone who makes a capital gain on their investment pays the same rate of tax. You will be taxed at the rate of thirty per cent on realised gains, but only after taking into account the following allowance:

(1)   The annual allowance. The first £5,900 (for 1985/86) of your net gains are exempted from tax, irrespective of the amount of gains made in any year (but this includes gains made by both husband and wife). The amount of the allowance is generally increased each year in line with increases in the cost of living.
(2)   Most capital losses which you realise can be deducted in arriving at your chargeable capital gains.
(3)   *Indexation.* A deduction can be made from the gain to take account of the effects of inflation on the gain and also on any loss.

(4)   Certain assets that produce capital gains are exempt from capital gains tax, ie Government Stock (held for over twelve months) and National Savings Certificates.

Clearly, the taxation of capital gains appears much more favourable than the profits or income derived from interest bearing investments. It is, therefore, sensible when planning your investments to take account of the differences so as to ensure that you suffer the lowest overall rate of tax. However, investment return is the most important requirement, you should never let the 'tax tail wave the investment dog'.

Inflation

Until recently, inflation faced investors with an unwelcome choice. If they selected investments to safeguard their capital, they faced the certainty that it would be gradually eroded as the purchasing power of money declined. If, on the other hand, they chose investments whose value increased to compensate for inflation, they ran the risk of a decline rather than increase. The traditional inflation hedges of equities and property are well known for the fact that their value can go down as well as up.

The chief sufferers from this were the small investors who are dependent upon their savings. As a result, it was to these people that the remedy of index linking was first made available. Unfortunately, the original index linked investments, granny bonds, were not particularly attractive. Despite this, large sums of money were put into them as their availability was widened. More recently, a much more attractive inflation protected investment has been made available in the form of index linked gilts. Initially, however, they could only be bought by pension funds. After a year the restriction was removed, and everyone is now free to buy index linked government stock. The result has been to give everyone the opportunity of complete protection against inflation. The potential of this is clearly very great, but so far few private investors have taken advantage of the opportunity.

Protection against inflation, plus a small real return is comparatively unexciting at a time when equities have risen 150 per cent over a few years. However it is doubtful that equities can keep up at this pace in the short term and index linked gilts are well worth considering (see the chapter on interest bearing investments).

Although inflation has receded as a threat, it certainly has not disappeared, and could easily re-emerge as the dominant investment consideration. Between 1976 and 1982, prices doubled. This meant that if your investment did not grow by more than 100 per cent, you could actually got poorer. As in *Alice Through the Looking Glass*, it took all the running you could do to stay in the same place.

If prices are stable, cash represents a safe, if unrewarding investment. In an inflationary world, this is not so. A pound tommorow will be worth less than a pound today. During the ten years to 1982 prices rose 200 per cent, and at the end of the period things cost three and a half times as much as they did in 1970. In other words, in 1982 you needed one pound to buy what could be purchased for 5s 11d in 1970. Some things have gone up even more. A London evening paper in 1970 cost 6d, while its successor in 1981 cost 17p — an increase of 580 per cent in eleven years. Although this appears an enormous increase, it actually represents an annual rate of price inflation of eighteen per cent. It takes very few years of double digit inflation to increase prices several hundred per cent.

There is no complete solution to the problem of inflation where the rate of price increases outstrips the return you can obtain on your investments. It is therefore important to ensure that, to as great a degree as possible, your investments are arranged in such a way as to produce the best return while retaining sufficient flexibility in order that they can be adapted to changing investment and inflation conditions.

12 Interest bearing investments

The great attraction of fixed income and fixed capital investment is that you know how much money you will have when
you need it. The drawback in an inflationary age is that you do
not know how much it will buy. Recently, this difficulty has
been overcome by the introduction of index linked securities.
The terms of these are fixed in relation to the cost of living
index, but currently suffer from the drawback that they produce a relatively low income.

Whatever your circumstances, you need to keep at least a part
of your assets in some form of fixed capital investment, even if
it is only a comparatively small reserve for the proverbial rainy
day. There is a great variety of this type of investment, but
there are few which offer the best solutions for the great
majority of investors. Nevertheless, there are attractive and
secure investments that are applicable to most investors and
we outline those that are most commonly used by the public as
a home for their savings.

Building societies

The most popular building society investment is the ordinary
share. The great attraction of this is that you can lay your hands
on your money whenever you want it. In addition, it pays a
competitive rate of interest. On the other hand, it is not at all
appropriate for a person who pays no income tax at all, since
he cannot reclaim the tax which the building society has paid.
The return on offer at the time of writing is 8.25 per cent with
the basic rate of tax already paid. You have to get 11.79 per cent
gross to receive the same return after tax. Although building
society ordinary shares are popular, they are not necessarily
the best place for retired people to keep a significant part of
their assets. If you can put in the money so that it is subject to

90 days' notice of withdrawal, you can earn as much as ten per cent per annum. In practice you are highly unlikely to need a large sum of money without any warning. Even if you do, the penalties are relatively modest, the loss of 90 days' interest may be outweighed by the extra interest that you have earned in the past few years. As a result, the advantage of immediate accessibility is of little use to retired people. They can do much better by tying their money up for a little longer.

Until recently, the terms offered by building societies were all much the same, although a few of the smaller ones offered slightly higher rates. Today, the situation has become much more competitive and it certainly makes sense to look around before deciding where to place your money. Once you have chosen a society you should regularly review the market in order to make sure that you can't do better elsewhere. A number of newspapers and financial magazines publish surveys of building society investment from time to time. It is still generally true that the best terms are available from some of the smaller specialist societies. They are able to offer them because they tend to provide higher priced mortgages.

Certain investors shy away from putting money into a small society. It is doubtful whether this is a sensible reaction if it is a member of the Building Societies Association. In the past, when one of the members has got into trouble, the others have rallied round and protected the investors from loss.

Government stock

Government stock, or 'gilts' are almost certainly the most attractive of interest bearing investments; they are also one of the least used as far as the private investor is concerned. There are a large number of different issues of government stock, each of which has its own unique characteristics. Most of them are either due to be redeemed on a fixed date or within a certain period of time. The attraction for the government of having a certain amount of latitude over the timing is that it can choose to redeem the stock when conditions are favourable. If it is tied to a fixed date, the money must be repaid regardless of the circumstances. The stock is normally denominated in units of £100 and this is the amount which will be repaid on redemption.

In addition to a repayment date, the stock pays interest and this is normally done every six months. The rate of interest varies greatly from one issue to another. Some stock is known as having a high coupon, and this may be ten, eleven or twelve per cent whereas other issues are known as low coupon stocks and this may be three, four or five per cent.

As well as differences in yield, the issues of government stock have different redemption dates. Some are due to be repaid within a matter of months whereas others won't be repaid until well into the next century. Stocks with less than five years to redemption are known as 'shorts' and those with between five and fifteen years are known as 'mediums'. Over fifteen years defines a 'long'. There are even a few issues of 'undated' stock which may never be redeemed.

Government stocks are traded on The Stock Exchange and their value is liable to fluctuate. Clearly, the value of any one stock is unlikely to be far from the par value of £100 when it is due to be redeemed for this amount within a matter of months. On the other hand, if redemption is many years in the future the value of the stock can fluctuate considerably as interest rates move.

When other interest rates are high, government stock will fall in value so as to produce a matching return. As rates fall, the stock will rise. The greatest fluctuations are seen in undated stock and those with redemption dates which are far in the future. For this reason, those who wish to minimise the risks they are running are well advised to restrict their investments to the short dated issues which are conventionally taken to be those whose redemption is more than five years ahead.

The prices of gilt edged stock are shown in the leading newspapers and beside them will be found different figures indicating the return which is available to an investor. These may differ from the nominal interest which the stock pays. The reason for this is that the price is likely to be considerably removed from the par value of £100. It may be either higher or lower. If it is below par, it means that those who hold these stocks until redemption can expect to receive a capital gain in addition to the income that will be paid on the stock. Set out below are examples of several typical issues:

Annual returns after tax deductions (where applicable)					
	No tax	30%	40%	50%	60%
Shorts					
Treasury 3% 1987 (85 $\frac{3}{8}$)	9.67	8.69	8.36	8.03	7.71
Treasury 12% 1987 (101 $\frac{13}{16}$)	11.23	7.44	6.18	4.92	3.67
Mediums					
Treasury 13% 1990 (105 $\frac{7}{8}$)	11.32	7.60	6.36	5.11	3.87
Funding 5 $\frac{3}{4}$% 1987/91 (82 $\frac{1}{4}$)	9.94	7.88	7.20	6.52	5.84
Longs					
Treasury 13 $\frac{3}{4}$% 2000/3					
(118 5/16)	11.14	7.55	6.33	5.12	3.89
Funding 3 $\frac{1}{2}$% 1999/2004 (47 $\frac{3}{4}$)	9.37	7.63	7.07	6.51	5.96

The first stock shown, Treasury three per cent 1987, would cost £85 $\frac{3}{8}$ for every £100 'nominal'. This will provide an income of £3 a year ie interest of 3.51 per cent on the purchase price.

In addition, the buyer will receive a guaranteed £100 sometime in 1987 (the actual redemption date varies from stock to stock; in this case it happens to be 14/7/87). The increase in value from £85 $\frac{3}{8}$ to £100 can clearly be expressed as an annual rate of growth and this when combined with the 3.51 per cent interest equates to an overall investment return of 9.67 per cent gross.

The £3 is taxable and so the net yield at different tax rates is also shown.

The next stock will also be redeemed in 1987 (3/11/87 to be precise). In this case, however, the stock pays a higher level of income and the price of the stock reflects this. Anybody buying this stock is looking purely for income because they will incur a capital loss if they hold on to it until redemption.

This produces a higher nominal return for non taxpayers but a lower one for those paying tax at the basic rate or above. The reason for this is that the two returns from the investment are taxed differently. Income from government stock is taxed in exactly the same way as from any other source. Capital gains, in contrast, are tax-free provided the stock has been held for more than a year. As a result, there is a considerable demand from high rate taxpayers for stock which stands at a discount from its redemption value and will in consequence produce a capital gain rather than income.

A similar pattern exists with the longer dated issues. After a time the prospect of redemption ceases to have any real effect of the stock's price, all that matters is the income which it produces. These stocks and, in particular, the undated issues are bought by those who believe that interest rates are likely to fall so that they can make a capital gain. In the meantime, they enjoy the comparatively high running yield available. Thus the funding 3.5 per cent standing at £48 $\frac{1}{4}$ produces an annual return of 7.25 per cent on the money invested in contrast to the less than half this amount available from the short dated stock.

Index-linked gilts

Public interest was limited when index-linked gilts were originally introduced. One reason for this was that the private investor was not able to buy them. This was quickly changed but they were still of limited appeal since there was not much choice of stock. This has now been rectified and there are no less than ten different index-linked government stocks with redemption dates ranging from 1988 to 2020.

The index-linked government stock or 'gilts' work in exactly the same way as conventional ones except that the redemption payment (and the interest paid in the meantime) is adjusted to take account of the fall in the value of money. The adjustment effectively increases their value by the rise in the Retail Price Index. The value of this naturally depends much upon the rate of inflation which we are going to experience. If it is negligible then the value of the inflation protection is small. If the economy does less well, it will be correspondingly enhanced.

Although the redemption value and the interest are index-linked this does not mean that the security will retain the same real value all the time. It is traded on The Stock Exchange and its price will vary according to demand, just as that of any other government stock does. If you buy stock and hold it to redemption you know exactly what return you will get in terms of real purchasing power.

If you sell it in the interim, you may do either better or worse, depending upon how the market has moved in the meantime.

During the few years this stock has been in existence, it has been much less affected by changes in interest rates than are conventional gilts. At the present price levels all the index-linked stocks promise a running yield (annual income) of around 2.25–2.75 per cent in real terms. Allowing for the additional capital gain to redemption, real returns vary from a total of over four per cent on the shortest stocks to three per cent on the longer issues.

It is difficult to compare an index-linked investment with a conventional one. It all depends on what the rate of inflation will be in the future, and no one knows this. If we assume future price rises of around 7.5 per cent per annum the index-linked stock offers a return of around eleven per cent. This is more or less in line with what you can get if you buy a conventional gilt. Of course at present inflation is not as high as this and this is one reason why the short dated index-linked stock has a higher rate of return. The stock due to be redeemed in 1988 provides a real redemption yield of nearly five per cent.

Summary

The attraction of an interest bearing investment is that it is certain. Investors often overrate the advantages of liquidity and can frequently obtain a significantly better rate of return if their money is tied up for a certain period. This is particularly true with building society investment. Government stock is an attractive investment for all classes of investor. It can be purchased either through a stockbroker, a bank or in most cases through the Post Office (in which case the interest is paid without deduction of tax). It is important to choose the right stock to obtain the highest possible return net of tax. Index-linked gilts offer protection against inflation but in return they give a comparatively small nominal income. Of course the value of this increases as time goes by.

One or two other types of fixed-interest investments are also worth mentioning.

Offshore roll-up funds

We have previously mentioned how these operate (see p 92) and the way in which taxable income is deferred until the investor realises his investment. These funds are for all practical purposes the equivalent of having funds on deposit in the Isle of Man and the Channel Islands and the tax treatment makes them most attractive. An investor could, for example, use an investment in such a fund to take an annual 'income', much of which will be tax free.

Example 9

An investor has £100,000 in a sterling fund which achieves growth of twelve per cent per annum. If he draws £12,000 each year the following amounts will be subject to income tax:

Year 1	1,285	Year 6	5,921
Year 2	2,434	Year 7	6,572
Year 3	3,459	Year 8	7,154
Year 4	4,374	Year 9	7,673
Year 5	5,191	Year 10	8,136

This effect arises because the amount charged under Sched 20 of the Finance Act 1984 is the gain computed according to capital gains tax principles. Thus the gains in year 1 are computed as follows:

	£
Sale proceeds	12,000
Cost $\dfrac{12,000}{12,000 + 100,000} \times £100,000$	10,715
Gain	1,285

National Savings

In recent years the government has placed a good deal of emphasis on keeping the rates of interest offered on the various national savings plans competitive with their market rivals. It is now possible to obtain a commercial return and enjoy complete security of capital by investing in this way. In addition, national savings are one of the few investments that pay interest without deduction of tax at source.

National Savings Income Bonds

Interest is paid on a monthly basis without deduction of tax. The interest rate is variable and subject to notice of change. You may cash part of your holding in multiples of £1,000, but you must keep a minimum of £2,000 invested. There are stringent penalties if you wish to redeem all or part of your capital at short notice which could mean forfeiting some or all of the interest.

National Savings Deposit Bonds

This is a relatively recent addition to the National Savings range and is designed to attract those who like an interest bearing investment which capitalises the interest rather than paying it as income. As with the Income Bond, interest is credited gross. Repayment is at three months' notice but there is an interest penalty if the investment is redeemed within one year of purchase.

National Savings Certificates

(Fixed interest variety). No interest is paid, but after a stated period, usually five years, the certificates can be redeemed at a higher value than the issue price. Certificates may be encashed with an increased value after one year, but the rate of increase is progressive and the full return can only be obtained by holding the certificates for the full term. The capital gain is free of all tax.

These certificates can also be used to produce an income. In effect this can be achieved by cashing a specified number of certificates each year to cream off the appreciation and at the end of the period the remaining certificates will repay the original investment. As the gain is tax free this can be extremely tax efficient means of providing spendable income for the higher rate taxpayer.

Example 10

30th issue yielding 8.85 per cent if held for five years:

Investment of £5,000.00

End of year	Certificates cashed	Income	Interest %
1	14	373.66	7.47
2	14	401.66	8.03
3	14	436.38	8.72
4	14	480.06	9.60
5	13	496.73	9.93

Remaining certificates repay £5,005.00

This exercise can be undertaken with most issues, and the number of certificates encashed is approximately the same in each case.

Index-Linked National Savings Certificates

Provided the certificates are held for more than a year the redemption value is equal to the original purchase price, increased in proportion to the RPI which has occurred between the month of the purchase and the month of redemption. In addition to the index linking holders can also receive a supplementary payment, and at the end of five years a further bonus is also payable on encashment. Once again, the capital gain is free of all taxes.

Annuities

The traditional investment for a retired person used to be an annuity. In its usual form you pay a lump sum to an insurance company, which then promises to pay you an income for however long you live.

The payments made under an annuity depend on two factors:

(1)   interest rates generally available at the time you purchase the annuity
(2)   your age at the time you start the annuity.

If you are, say, sixty-five when you buy your annuity you can expect a life expectancy of about thirteen years. The insurance company constructs the annuity to repay the capital to you over those thirteen years and pay interest on the outstanding capital. The repayments (which therefore consist partly of repaid capital and interest) are calculated so that they are equal payments for the rest of your life.

As a result, for any given purchase price, an annuity is higher for older people (and it will obviously be higher if interest rates at the time are high). On the other hand annuities for women are lower because all the available evidence shows that women live longer than men.

The interest 'element' is taxed at source but the tax can be reclaimed if you are a non tax-payer.

There is a wide variety of annuities and you can arrange to have the income paid every month, quarter, half year or year. You can also buy an annuity which will pay out a certain minimum amount, regardless of whether you survive. One arrangement which is particularly popular is the so called capital protected annuity. In this, the insurance company guarantees to return the purchase price of the annuity, either in a series of payments while you are alive, or by making up the difference by a lump sum when you die. A pension is a form of annuity and this is usually arranged on the basis of monthly payments with a guaranteed minimum of five years' income.

Annuity contracts are irrevocable. If they were not, anyone who had bought one would endeavour to surrender it as soon as there was any sign of his health deteriorating. This the insurance company cannot allow since it depends on the profits which it makes from those who die early to pay for the losses which it makes on those who live longer than expected. It is this pooling of risk which makes the annuity so useful. It enables the insurance company to pay out a higher proportion of capital each year than would be prudent for an individual to select himself. Unfortunately, this irrevocability makes annuities unsuitable investments for young people. The danger of a revival of inflation is simply too great. Many people who bought annuities twenty years ago when they were sixty-five found that their income had lost two thirds of its purchasing power within little more than a decade.

The fact remains that annuities offer the highest possible continuing income. The older you are, the better will be the return and a seventy-five old man could get more than £200 a year for an investment of £1,000. The time to use annuities is once a man is past seventy and a woman over seventy-five. Many insurance companies offer annuities which increase the amount paid out each year or two. These are generally not worth buying since the tax free content does not rise and the initial return is greatly reduced in order to make possible the higher payouts later on.

Annuity home income schemes

It is undoubtedly true that many people invest considerable sums in their homes on the grounds that in retirement the property can be sold and part of the proceeds used to spend in retirement. It is also undoubtedly true that many people who do so eventually decide to stay in their home and consequently find their cash resources lower than they would wish. For these people one answer to their problem is to use their home to provide spendable income and this can be done without suffering undue inconvenience. This can be achieved by arranging a home income scheme on the strength of the equity that has been built up in the property. Essentially the scheme works like this:

(1)   The home owner takes a mortgage on the property up to £30,000 on an 'interest only' basis. Tax relief is gained on the interest provided that at least ninety per cent of the amount raised is used to buy an annuity.
(2)   The home owner purchases an annuity which is sufficient to cover the interest on the mortgage and leave enough to provide additional spendable income.
(3)   When the home-owner (or owners where there is a couple) dies the house is sold and the mortgage is repaid — the sale proceeds less the outstanding mortgage form part of the deceased's estate.

Certain conditions must be met before such a scheme can be arranged, and generally they are applicable only to the very elderly. In the case of a single person they normally have to be at least seventy years of age, and a married couple must have a combined age of 150.

As an example of the level of income that can be produced, a seventy-five year old woman arranging a £25,000 loan would receive spendable income of £1,411 if she pays tax at the basic rate. The scheme can be adapted to those who wish to raise some capital as well as receive an income.

Provided you are in the right age bracket and you have a property worth more than £15,000 then you could consider such a scheme. It represents a useful way of using capital 'locked away' in your property and the use of a loan in this way reduces the value of your estate for CTT purposes.

Insurance company funding schemes

These insurance policy based schemes comprise two separate parts:

(1)   Temporary annuity (see p 127 for an explanation of an annuity)
(2)   Endowment assurance policy for ten years

Most of your capital investment is applied to purchase a temporary annuity providing a level income. The annuity payments may be made yearly, (starting one year from the date you start your plan) or monthly (commencing one month after the starting date), and will be made directly to your bank account.

The balance of your capital investment is the first premium on the endowment assurance policy. The second and subsequent premiums are met from the net annuity payments and will normally be paid by direct debiting mandate from your bank account.

The combination of annuity and endowment bond will provide:

Income

The payments from the annuity not used to fund the regular premiums are available as net income.

Capital

The proceeds of the endowment assurance policy at the end of the period are payable to you either as a tax free cash sum, or you may choose to take a tax free income from the proceeds.

There is no guarantee that the amount repaid by the insurance company at the end of the ten years will equal the original investment. This is dependent on current bonus levels remaining the same as they are today and of course these may well reduce. Nevertheless, there is a degree of protection against this happening in that the scheme can be set up taking into account a lower bonus rate. In this case the income is lower but in the event of bonuses remaining at the level they are today there would be a capital gain at the end of ten years. This gain would be free of all tax.

It is of course important to undestand that in order to obtain the full benefit from this type of plan it has to be maintained for the full ten years.

13 Capital growth investments

Until index-linked gilts were introduced, interest bearing investment provided no protection against inflation. Even now, the role which they can fill is limited and they certainly do not provide any mechanism by which you can share in the increasing wealth of the country. As a result, the basis of any long-term growth investment plan must be equities and/or property based. During the 1970s, many observers favoured putting the greater weight upon property. In the last few years, the pendulum has swung back to favouring equities. This seems to be largely a reaction to the way the different types of investment have performed.

In the four years up to the end of 1984, British equities rose by 150 per cent while a typical group of properties rose by something like 50 per cent. In the five years up to the beginning of 1978, the typical equity portfolio with income reinvested showed a return of only twenty per cent over the whole period, while a typical group of properties increased by thirty per cent or more.

Whether you are investing in equities or property, you will need to follow similar principles. The most important rule is to diversify your investment. This simply means not putting all your eggs in one basket. Both types of investment carry risks, and it is unnecessarily foolhardy to leave yourself completely exposed to an isolated piece of bad luck. In 1960 few shares were more highly regarded than Rolls Royce yet this did not stop the company failing ten years later. There are many similar though less well-known examples of property investments which proved equally unrewarding.

Until less than twenty years ago, it was difficult for anyone except the very rich to acquire a diversified investment in a number of properties. The reason for this was simply their cost. If a person was going to buy even half a dozen properties, he had to restrict himself to comparatively small ones, and even then would have tied up several hundred thousand pounds in present day money. It is unlikely that he would want to do this, since many of the most attractive investment opportunities are in larger, more expensive property.

In contrast, the medium-sized investor had no trouble in obtaining a well-diversified portfolio of ordinary shares. He could put either a few hundred or few thousand pounds into each of a dozen or so companies. Alternatively, he could purchase the shares of an investment trust which itself held shares in many different companies. If he took advantage of this method of spreading his risk, he had to deal with a complicating factor. This is that the shares of investment trusts, just like those of any other company dealt with on The Stock Exchange, fluctuate in accordance with supply and demand. The result if sentiment moved against the investment trust could be for its share price to fall even though the value of the underlying securities rose. Alternatively, if demand for the trust's shares increased, their price could rise even if the underlying assets declined.

Just as investment trusts were set up to provide a ready made diversified investment in equities, property companies were set up to do the same in their field. The situation was, however, rather different since the property companies were often managed in a much more entrepreneurial way than investment trusts. They were frequently highly geared and as a result made considerable development profits. Attractive as these investments were, they were hardly a substitute for a direct stake in bricks and mortar.

The 1960s saw the rise of the unit trust movement. This made it possible for even the smallest investor to obtain a stake in a diversified and managed portfolio of ordinary shares. Due to legal technicalities, it was not possible for unit trusts which invest in property to be offered to the public. It was, however, a comparatively short time before a way was found of achieving the same end by using the medium of a life assurance policy. The introduction of the property bond opened up a new dimension of investment to the ordinary person.

Equities

Ordinary shares, or equities as they are more commonly termed, are a company's risk capital; the investor who buys them expects a reasonable and rising level of dividend income and also a rise in the share price, but there is no certainty of either. If his expectations are fulfilled, then he is rewarded for taking the risk that the company might have encountered trading problems and that dividends might have fallen and the share price slumped. It is this risk which separates equities from other commonly held investments such as National Savings Certificates, building society shares and government stock. Where a person takes a risk with his capital he expects a higher than average return and historically this has proved to be the case.

In a recent study by stockbrokers de Zoete and Bevan it is revealed that equities have given a positive real return in forty of the last sixty-six years. Allowing for the reinvestment of gross income there is no period of twenty years or more since 1919 in which equities have failed to give a positive real return. The average real return since 1919 has been seven per cent per annum.

This performance compares favourably with that of building society shares as the following table illustrates:

Funds invested in equities and building society shares (with net income reinvested)

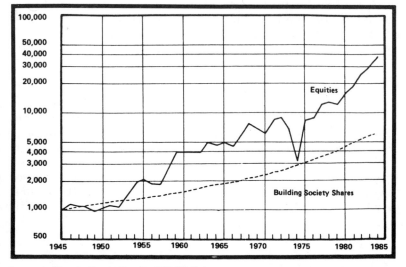

(source: The de Zoete Equity-Gilt Study)

Not only do equities provide capital growth, but they are also a long-term means of generating income. Equity dividends increased by fifteen per cent in real terms in 1984, the third successive year of real dividend increase. If, as is widely forecast, the real value of dividends increase in 1985 this would be the longest unbroken run of real dividend growth since the equity bull markets of the 1920s and 1930s.

While the table shows how well equities have performed in the long term, it also clearly demonstrates what can happen to share prices during a period of economic difficulties, as was experienced in the 1970s. As we have mentioned in previous chapters, personal circumstances will dictate whether an investment in equities is suitable for you, but from the information we have it is clear that an exposure to The Stock Market is desirable for most investors, at least to a limited extent.

Your own portfolio

There is no reason at all why you cannot run your portfolio yourself if you want to. Indeed, if you enjoy investment and are able to devote the time to it, then you may be lucky and do much better for yourself than you will by pooling your assets with others and having them handled by professional investment managers. Despite this, investment is not an easy matter and is extremely time consuming if done properly. In addition, the pooled funds handled by professional managers do possess some important tax advantages. As a result an increasing number of people have chosen to use unit trusts and similar devices rather than handling their own portfolio.

Unit trusts

Unit trusts provide a vehicle by which a number of different investors can pool their assets to buy shares. It permits existing investors to sell out and new ones to come in with no difficulty. The organisation of a unit trust is undertaken by a management company which is also responsible for choosing investments. The assets themselves are held by a trustee, who makes sure that the interests of the investors are taken care of. This structure has worked so well that there has never been a unit trust failure.

Suppose a manager collects £1 million to start a trust. He decides to invest in equal amounts in two companies, both of whose shares stand at £2.

Investment in company A   250,000 shares @ £2

Investment in company B   250,000 shares @ £2

Total investment £1,000,000

His investors between them now hold one million units of £1 each — the precise number of units each has depends on how much they invested in the first place.

Suppose now at the next valuation, shares in company A are now £3 whereas shares in B are still £2. The total investment is now worth £1.25m and each unit has increased in value to £1.25. If *new* investors wish to joint the trust, this is the price (the offer price) at which they buy in. If existing investors wish to sell units, the manager agrees to buy these from them for a slightly lower price (the bid price). This price difference covers the costs of running the unit trust.

Types of fund

When unit trusts started there were only three types of fund recognised generally. These were income, general and growth funds, and corresponded to the main needs of different classes of investor.

The objective of the growth fund is to seek to achieve the greatest possible capital appreciation. Managing an income fund is rather less straightforward. The object is to secure a high income for investors. A successful income trust will aim primarily to produce a steadily rising flow of distribution and will only be concerned with capital performance as a secondary consideration.

In a general trust, both capital and income get equal weight. This means that the managers may accept a cut in income if this would seem likely to produce a more than commensurate improvement in the capital performance. On the other hand, they would certainly not totally disregard the interests of those who bought units in order to enjoy the distributions from them. If the income fell at one point, they would generally expect to restore it at the earliest opportunity.

Today, the situation has become much more complicated. The Unit Trust Association now has more than 700 different unit trusts divided into no fewer than fifteen different categories.

Sector index performance to 28 February 1985
Investment of £100 at the beginning of the period

	1 year	3 year	5 year
UK general	123.3	204.6	270.7
UK growth	120.9	203.2	265.8
UK equity income	123.2	206.9	252.8
UK mixed income (pref/equity)	119.2	197.9	226.2
North American	141.6	230.5	310.4
Far Eastern	122.7	197.2	290.6
Japan	134.6	259.8	457.2
Australia	89.7	122.8	108.7
Europe	124.4	223.3	266.2
International	124.7	213.5	272.1
Commodity & energy	94.5	149.2	141.3
Finance & property shares	120.2	188.1	257.1
Investment trust units	125.7	213.9	318.0
Gilt & fixed interest growth	104.3	154.2	173.3
Gilt & fixed interest income	103.0	145.3	159.6

(source: *Money Management* March 1985)

The sector index performance figures beside each class of fund show the average performance of all the trusts in the group. They are calculated by reinvesting the net income after tax in the purchase of further units so as to permit an overall comparison of the different types of fund.

Interesting as past performance figures may be, it is important not to exaggerate their significance. What matters to you is their performance *in the future*, not what happened last week, last year or a decade ago. The most that the past can do is give a rough guide to the future and you must accept that you are unlikely to choose the best performing trust. Your aim should be to make certain that you don't get one of the worst. This means looking for one of the better established groups, since their performance is unlikely to be extreme.

Investment bonds

These are lump sum investments issued by life assurance companies. They cover a broad range of investments and through them it is possible to invest in properties, equities, gilt-edged securities, interest bearing investments and so on. There are also combined funds which invest in a range of different types of investment (typically a combination of property, equity and interest bearing investments). These combined funds (or managed funds) have been very popular since their introduction in the early 1970s.

The insurance company will specify the minimum initial investment which it will accept in a bond, and this is typically £1,000. Sometimes they will allow a smaller additional investment, but even then the amount is likely to be £500. The charges are similar to those levied by unit trusts, being usually a combination of an initial charge (the difference between the offer and bid price) levied when your money goes in and a recurring one. Typically the initial charge is five per cent (plus a rounding amount) together with an annual management charge of 0.75 per cent per annum.

Although there is a minimum initial investment, you are normally free to make regular withdrawals from the fund even if this means that you fall below the minimum level. This is necessary because the bonds do not normally distribute the income which they earn but reinvest it within the fund. Many bonds allow you to specify how much you wish to withdraw at any one time although most of them fix a minimum withdrawal of £50. It is customary for the insurance companies to allow you to switch between one fund and another without charge or after payment of a nominal amount.

In structure, investment bonds are similar to unit trusts. They are 'pooled' investments and the individual investor's holding is represented by units which rise and fall in value in line with the value of the underlying investments.

However, there are points of difference between the taxation of a direct investment in a unit trust and one which is channelled through an investment bond. Most of them are of minor significance, but there are one or two of real importance although they only matter to those who pay tax at the higher rate. The situation of a basic rate taxpayer is more or less the same whether his investment is in a bond or unit trust.

The most important point for higher rate taxpayers is that any gain they make in a bond is liable to higher rate tax. The only exception to this is that you are allowed to take out five per cent of your initial investment for each year in which you have been investing in the bond up till a maximum of twenty years. Thus, after ten years you can take out fifty per cent of your initial investment. Alternatively, you may take out five per cent each year.

Provided you don't overtake the five per cent annual allowance, the higher rate tax is not levied until the bond is cashed. This means that it can be a useful means of tax planning, since you can put off cashing the bond until a year in which your income is low. When a bond is cashed, the gain is divided by the number of years during which it has been in force. This amount is then added to your income and the additional tax calculated. This tax rate is then applied to the whole of the gain. Thus if you had a gain of £4,000 in the bond and had held it for eight years, £500 would be added to your income. If this additional income was taxed at sixty per cent, the basic rate would be subtracted from it to give a rate of thirty per cent which would be applied to the whole gain from the bond. The net gain would only be £2,800. This would obviously be thoroughly tax inefficient if the profit was a product of capital gains rather than reinvested income.

Types of fund

Property funds have also been a popular investment, unique to insurance companies. Just as unit trusts are invested in the shares of companies, property bonds put their money into offices, factories and other buildings. The size of property bond funds varies very greatly, with the biggest worth over £500m and some of them only a few hundred thousand pounds. This difference in size is much more significant for property bonds than it is for equity funds. There are considerable advantages in running a small portfolio of ordinary shares. In contrast, a large property bond fund is considerably easier to manage than a small one.

Many of the best investment opportunities involve the purchase or development of large office blocks. These cost many millions of pounds and there is no way in which they can be afforded by the small fund. In addition, the large funds have usually got that way by growing over many years. This means that the inflow of new money is a comparatively small proportion of the total fund. Many small funds are new and in contrast their inflow of new money is frequently a high proportion of the fund.

It can take a long time to negotiate the purchase of a property and it is difficult to judge in advance how much a property fund will have to invest. As a result, if money flows in faster than expected, a small fund may find itself with almost as much of its assets in cash as in property. This may or may not produce a reasonable investment result but it is certainly not the object of investing in a property bond. Similar considerations apply to the possiblity of investors liquidating their holdings. A small property bond fund has to maintain a higher degree of liquidity because it has a much smaller selection of properties to sell if holdings are redeemed.

Most insurance funds are invested in equities, and very often there is a choice of specialised funds, eg UK equities, international equities and so on.

Not only do insurance companies link their bonds to equities, they also have fixed interest and gilt funds. The guilt funds are liable to fluctuate with the market in government stocks. In contrast the money funds are effectively put on deposit and their objective is stability. As a result, they produce a steady return, but one which is usually less than that of a gilt fund.

Their function in insurance bonds is to complement the equity and property funds. It is usually possible for investors to switch between one fund and another at minimal cost. There are occasions when neither equities nor property appear attractive and then the fixed interest fund provides an ideal temporary home for a person's investment.

Managed funds

The traditional spread of investments includes equities, property and fixed interest investments. The proportions vary according to the judgment of the investment manager and the objectives of the fund. Insurance companies offer a combination of these as the complete answer to the person who wants the broadest possible spread of investment. This arrangement has a number of different names but is most commonly known as a 'managed' fund. Virtually every significant unit-linked insurance company offers one and some of them have become extremely popular. The largest has some £750m in it, and there are many managed funds with over £100m.

There are a variety of reasons for this popularity. Although equities have produced spectacular performance in the last few years, showing a rise of 150 per cent over five years, they are liable to violent fluctuation. Property is much more stable but has only shown an increase of fifty five to sixty per cent over the same period. Managed funds have succeeded in combining the two forms of investment and have produced a typical rise of just over 100 per cent. This combination of steadiness with performance is the answer for many investors. It is particularly important to avoid wide fluctuations when you are gradually running down your capital. This is the position of many retired people so that managed funds appeal particularly to them.

14 A sensible investment strategy for the prudent investor

Neither this book nor any other will pick out the best performing investments for you. If anyone were able to do this, they would certainly take good care to keep the information to themselves and certainly would not spend their time writing books on the subject! This is not so true with managed funds and unit trusts; some groups do consistently perform better than average. You will need to do this research yourself; look through *Money Management* or *Planned Savings* for insurance and unit trust groups which regularly feature amongst the ten leading funds, in each specialist sector.

There are certain principles which should be considered by all investors when forming a portfolio, and therefore we offer some suggestions as a guide for those who prefer to take on board the responsibility of making their own investment decisions.

Investment strategy

Your approach to investment should be controlled by an investment policy, formulated in the light of your personal circumstances. This policy should include the following criteria:

(1) there should be access to part of your capital;
(2) the capital should be spread across a number of different types of investment, each depending on how long you can tie up the money;
(3) undue risk should be avoided as far as possible — including the possibility of a significant reduction in interest rates;
(4) a degree of flexibility is desirable to allow switching from one type of asset to another;
(5) the portfolio should reflect the fact that spendable

income can be produced by capital growth as well as dividend or interest income. Higher rates of tax, if relevant, should be considered at all times;

(6)   never forget inflation, even at the relatively modest levels of today. It is all too easy to opt for the investment that produces the highest income at the start, only to find later that the real value of your capital has fallen appreciably. The following graph shows how this has happened.

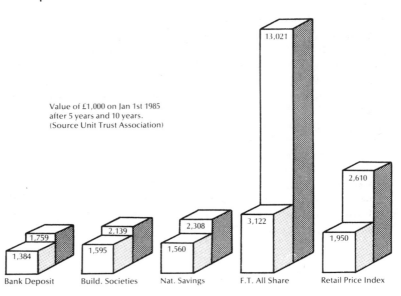

Value of £1,000 on Jan 1st 1985 after 5 years and 10 years. (Source Unit Trust Association)

Bank Deposit	Build. Societies	Nat. Savings	F.T. All Share	Retail Price Index
1,384 / 1,759	1,595 / 2,139	1,560 / 2,308	3,122 / 13,021	1,950 / 2,610

Cash flow

Any portfolio that is established with the primary objective of producing spendable income should be arranged in such a way as to produce a regular and even cash flow. Few retired people will wish to receive their income on an annual or half yearly basis. Income should be as regular as practicable, and the choice of investment should reflect this requirement, although it should not be the overriding factor when making the final decision.

It's impossible to say how much should go into any particular type of investment, as each portfolio will be arranged to suit individual circumstances. However, most people will not want

to immediately lock all their money up in long-term investments, but rather will take the view that part should be kept for
short-term use, some may be needed after five years, and the
balance can be salted away for long-term investment. By adopt-
ing this approach, certain categories of investment will automatically select themselves.

Within three years

This is the cash you just feel you might need in the next couple
of years. Some will need to be available immediately — the
remainder can be on longer-term deposit to obtain a higher
return. You must ask yourself:

How much money do you feel should be immediately access-
ible? £500? £1,000? Whatever amount you feel is right should go
into your building society, or into one of the interest bearing
current accounts, which allows withdrawals without notice.

How much more do you feel comfortable about being available
at, say three months' notice? Perhaps you would feel easier in
your mind if you were able to fund holidays and contingencies
(eg a major repair to the car) over the next two or three years.
That's the amount that should go into a building society offering the best rates you can find, which will normally entail having to give notice.

What this will provide is a cushion against unexpected emer-
gencies, and a cushion against adverse investment conditions
elsewhere. It will also enable you to plan your other investments without worrying about whether you will have the
money. On the other side of the coin, a float will provide the
means to take an unexpected investment opportunity. You will
also get a high level of income.

Three to five years

This is the money you will feel happier about if you know its
going to be back in your hands within five years. As this is still a
relatively short period you should put the money required during this period into gilts and National Savings.

Gilts: Even though, at the time of writing, real interest rates are
historically high, there is the possibility that over the medium
term these will fall. High coupon gilts offer a flexible means of

guaranteeing a fixed income for a pre-determined period. If interest rates do fall, it may be possible to sell the stock and make a tax free capital gain.

For those who do not need income, there is a choice of gilts that will produce guaranteed capital growth. These are the low coupon stocks, which stand at a price below the redemption value; or the index-linked stocks where the value is increased in line with inflation. Both are useful vehicles for providing a safe and risk free home for short-term capital.

National Savings Certificates: The tax exempt nature of this investment, and the competitive returns they offer, make them particularly attractive to the higher rate taxpayer. Like gilts, they can be purchased on the basis of a fixed return, or an index linked basis.

As explained earlier, National Savings Certificates can be used to provide the investor with capital growth or income.

More than five years

This is where equities, and equity-based investments such as unit trusts and/or investment bonds come into the reckoning (indeed they are longer-term investments and you shouldn't be looking at them as shorter-term investments). Invest for *income* if that's what you need, but look forward to capital growth over the long term as well.

It is perfectly possible to construct a portfolio of unit trusts specifically designed to provide you with an income. Unit trusts make income payments every six months; six unit trusts packaged together can therefore provide a monthly income. These 'monthly income plans' are marketed by the major companies and are increasingly used to supplement income in retirement.

The capital value of the investment will fluctuate (one only has to look back to 1974) but the overall level of dividend income from a widely spread portfolio of shares (which is what a unit trust is) has remained remarkably steady over the years.

Units trusts have tended to be looked at as purely capital investments. They are not — they are being used more and more to provide income with the very real prospect of capital growth over the longer term as well.

Used as a vehicle to provide income and capital growth, the managed bond can also play a useful and rewarding role. This is especially true where the investor is a higher rate taxpayer at the time the bond is established, but his rate of tax has reduced to the basic rate when the bond is encashed.

A judicious combination of these investments should fulfil all the criteria laid down in our investment policy. As a result, your investment returns should be good and much of the concern that is associated with investment should be eliminated. You will, of course, need to review the position regularly, to ensure that you are obtaining the best possible returns.

Taxation

You can't ignore taxation but you shouldn't let tax get in the way of a sound investment decision. However there is one area of taxation that you should make yourself familiar with and that's the age allowance because the tax rules contain a trap for those with a fairly modest income.

The age allowance is an Inland Revenue tax concession to those aged sixty-five or more during the tax year. Basically, the age allowance is a higher personal allowance and in the tax year 1985/86 this will be £2,690 for a single person and £4,255 for a married couple. This allowance, however, is reduced where total income exceeds £8,800, the allowance being reduced by £2 for every £3 of income above this sum. When total income reaches £10,000 per year the whole of the age allowance is lost.

Example 11

Married couple A with pension of £8,800 per year

Gross income	£8,800
Personal allowance (includes full age allowance)	4,255
Taxable income	£4,545

Tax at 30% on £4,545 *£1,363.50*

Net income £8,800 less 1,363.50 = £7,436.50

Married couple B with pension of £8,800 per year and 'grossed up' building society interest of £1,200 per year (£840 net of tax)

Gross income		£10,000
Personal allowance (includes full age allowance)	£4,255	
Less 2/3 income over £8,800 (ie 2/3 £1,200)	800	
Reduced personal allowance	£3,455	£3,455
Taxable income		£6,545

Tax at 30% on £6,545 = *£1,963.50*

Net income £10,000 less £1,963.50 = £8,036.50

Conclusion
The gross income of married couple B is £1,200 higher than married couple A but only £600 higher in net terms. Thus their building society interest has effectively been taxed at fifty per cent.

This problem can be overcome by switching the building society funds to a more tax efficient investment such as National Savings or a managed bond. Both could provide spendable income without the loss of age allowance.

Life assurance

When a person reaches the age of retirement it is generally thought that one of the last things that needs to be considered are additional life assurance policies. This need not be necessarily so, as in certain circumstances some form of life assurance contract can be useful.

Whole of life cover

There is probably a large number of people who have not yet made a will, and in the event of their death the surviving spouse may have limited funds on which to live until Letters of Administration are obtained. A life policy for a modest sum would not be out of order provided this is properly written on a 'life of another' basis with the wife as the owner of the policy (or written in trust for the benefit of the wife provided that the husband is not the only trustee). This will ensure a speedy settlement should a claim occur and the proceeds can be used as spendable capital until such times as the affairs of the estate are finalised. Similarly, obtaining probate can also be a lengthy process, and a life policy to cover this situation would also be advantageous.

Joint life cover

Specific policies have been designed to cover the CTT liability that may arise when an estate passes down to the next generation. These are arranged on the basis of joint lives, with husband and wife as the lives assured, the sum insured being paid on the second death. Provided the policy is properly written in trust for beneficiaries then the proceeds will fall outside the estate and will be free of tax. This can, in fact, be a simple and affordable means of ensuring that the assets built up during a lifetime are inherited by the next generation without having to be sold off in part to meet a CTT liability.

Endowment assurance

It is something of a misconception to believe that endowment policies are fifteen to twenty year term savings schemes that have no application to retired or semi-retired people. This is most definitely not true. Endowment policies can run for as little as five years, and the best returns are in fact obtained when the policy is issued on the basis of ten years' maximum term. These policies, known as 'maximum investment plans', can be issued to people up to the age of eighty-five, and are often used by retired people as a savings vehicle where there is a degree of surplus income. The returns on this type of policy are extremely competitive compared to other regular savings schemes, even when the policyholder is over the age of sixty.

Existing policies

If you find yourself in the fortunate position of having an endowment policy about to mature, think seriously about converting the policy to a whole of life insurance. This does not mean that you are tying up the proceeds until you die. Quite the reverse is in fact the case, as the policy is effectively transformed into a managed bond. The advantage of this process is quite simply that the proceeds can go on earning interest, or capital growth in the hands of the insurance company and this can be drawn off as income completely free of all personal tax. If a capital sum is required at any time then this can be withdrawn and the balance will go on earning interest. This facility is of particular advantage to higher rate taxpayers.

15 CTT planning: passing your wealth to your family

Capital transfer tax applies to most transfers of capital which take place either by way of lifetime gifts or by property passing on a death. The tax is charged at rates which progressively rise to a maximum rate of sixty per cent for transfers on death (or within three years of death) and 30 per cent in the case of lifetime gifts.

Band £000	Lifetime rates Rate %	Lifetime rates Cumulative tax £	Death rates Rate %	Death rates Cumulative tax £
0– 67	0	Nil	0	Nil
67– 89	15	3,300	30	6,600
89–122	$17\frac{1}{2}$	9,075	35	18,150
122–155	20	15,675	40	31,350
155–194	$22\frac{1}{2}$	24,450	45	48,900
194–243	25	36,700	50	73,400
243–299	$27\frac{1}{2}$	52,100	55	104,200
Over 299	30		60	

Originally, when CTT was introduced it was intended to be a lifetime tax with all transfers being taken into account, but in 1981 the Conservative Government introduced a ten year restriction to this rule. In other words, if you make a gift and survive ten years the slate is 'wiped clean' and the amount of your original Capital Transfer is left out of account in determining the CTT payable on subsequent occasions.

There are a number of exemptions and reliefs:

Transfers to your spouse

These are totally exempt except for the rather unusual situation where the donor is domiciled in the UK but the donee is not. In that case, the exemption is limited to £55,000.

This is clearly a very important exemption as it means that no CTT will be payable on property which you leave your wife.

Normal expenditure of income

There is also an exemption for gifts made out of income which are normal (ie habitual) expenditure and which do not eat into an individual's capital. This exemption usually covers gifts made by deed of covenant or premiums paid out of income on an insurance policy.

£250 exemption

There is an exemption for gifts not exceeding £250 for any one recipient in a tax year. The exemption is not available to cover part of a larger gift.

Annual £3,000 exemption

Lifetime gifts are exempt up to a total of £3,000 in any tax year, this limit being in addition to any number of gifts falling within the normal expenditure and the £250 exemptions. Both husband and wife qualify for this annual exemption. Where gifts fall short of the £3,000 limit the shortfall is carried forward to the following year and added to the allowance for that year only. Unused reliefs which have been carried forward from the previous year can only be utilised once the current year's annual exemption has been used.

Example 12

A made capital transfers in 1983/84 of £3,000. In 1984/85 he gave £5,000. Mrs A made transfers of £1,000 in 1982/83, £2,000 in 1983/84 and £5,000 in 1984/85.

The position is as follows:

	A	Mrs A
1982/83	N/A	exempt
1983/84	exempt	exempt
1984/85	£2,000 chargeable	£1,000 chargeable

Mrs A can utilise the balance of her 1983/84 allowance against her 1984/85 transfers, but she cannot carry forward the unused amount from 1982/83.

Exemption for marriage gifts

There is an exemption for gifts in consideration of a marriage. The amount of the exemption depends upon the relationship of the donor to the people being married. The exemptions are as follows:

£5,000   For a parent of either party to the marriage.
£2,500   By one party of the marriage to the other or by grandparents or great grandparents.
£1,000   In any other case.

The gift needs to be made *in consideration* of the marriage ie prior to and conditional upon the marriage or on the occasion of the marriage. Strictly speaking the exemption is not available for gifts which are made after the marriage has already taken place.

Gifts to charities

All gifts to registered charities are exempt whether they are made during lifetime or on death.

Gifts for national purposes

Gifts to certain national bodies are totally exempt. These include The National Gallery, The British Museum or any similar national institution, any museum or art gallery in the UK which is maintained by a local authority or university, The National Trust, any university or university college in the UK and any local authority or government department.

Gifts for public benefit

Gifts of eligible property to non-profit-making bodies are exempt provided specific Treasury consent is obtained. Eligible property includes land of outstanding historic, architectural or aesthetic interest, pictures, private books, manuscripts, works of art or collections of national scientific, historic or artistic interest.

Gifts to political parties

Gifts to qualifying political parties (those with at least two Members of Parliament elected at the last General Election, or at least one Member where the party had more than 150,000 votes cast for its candidates) are exempt, but the exemption is limited to £100,000 if the transfer is made on or within one year of death.

Business property and agricultural property

Business property relief or agricultural property relief may be available to reduce the amount of the capital transfer. These reliefs provide a deduction of either fifty per cent or thirty per cent in ascertaining the amount of the capital transfer before deduction of exemptions.

The rules which govern the rate of relief are as follows:

Business property relief

The fifty per cent deduction is given for a transfer of a sole trader's business assets, for a partner's interest in a firm's business, or for a controlling shareholding in a trading company. The thirty per cent deduction is given in respect of property owned by a partner or controlling shareholder and used by the firm or company (whether or not rent is charged) and for a minority shareholding in a trading company.

Certain trades do not qualify, ie trades dealing in securities and land. Furthermore, where a firm or company has investments, business property relief is restricted to the value of the partner's or shareholder's interest in assets *used in the trade*. However, the trade need not be carried on in the UK and shares in a foreign company may qualify for the relief.

It is normally necessary for the individual to have owned his business property for at least two years in order for the relief to be available.

Agricultural property relief

The fifty per cent relief is available for land occupied by the owner or by a firm in which he is a partner, and for tenanted land where the owner is entitled to obtain vacant possession within twelve months. In other circumstances the deduction is thirty per cent.

It is necessary for the land to be situated in the UK, Channel Islands or Isle of Man. Relief is given only in respect of agricultural land, but other assets of the farming business may attract business property relief.

Restriction on relief

If a loan is secured on business property or agricultural land, only the net amount after deduction of the loan ranks for relief. Thus if a farm worth £500,000 is subject to a £200,000 mortgage, only the balance of £300,000 attracts agricultural property relief. It would therefore be sensible to secure the borrowing on assets which do not attract agricultural property relief, though this may be difficult to achieve in practice.

Making the most of your exemptions

Giving away surplus income

Many older people feel quite comfortable about giving away surplus income on an *ad hoc* basis. Where there are grandchildren involved, the benefit to the recipient can be substantially increased if annual sums are paid under a deed of covenant. Older people are sometimes reluctant to take on a commitment to pay a fixed sum for seven years, but if they are able to enter into such a commitment £42.86 can be recovered on behalf of the grandchild for every £100 that is paid under a deed of covenant (provided the covenanted sums do not cause the child's personal allowance to be exceeded). This addition to the gift made by courtesy of the Inland Revenue will not cost the donor anything provided that the total of his payments under deed of covenant does not exceed his taxable income for the year.

Making use of the £3,000 exemption

Substantial sums may be transferred by making full use of this CTT exemption. Once again, the cost to the donor may be less than the value to the recipient. For example, it is possible for a person to give shares or securities on which there is a substantial unrealised capital gain and for a joint election to be made so that the capital gain is 'held over'. In other words, for Capital Gains Tax purposes these shares are deemed to be transferred at their original cost. If the recipient will not otherwise be making use of his annual £5,900 CGT exemption, it may be possible for him to realise the capital gain without CGT being payable.

Example 13

A (who has already used his CGT annual exemption) has shares which are worth £3,000 but which cost only £500. If he were to sell them he would have a capital gain of £2,500 (ignoring indexation), and tax of around £750 would be payable. If A were instead to give the shares to his son, he could 'hold over' the capital gain so that the son would be deemed to have acquired them for £500. A would not then be liable for CGT and the son could escape CGT by realising the investment in a year in which he had not used his annual £5,900 CGT exemption.

Taking advantage of the ten year rule

If tax saving is the main consideration, and a person is sufficiently wealthy, it clearly makes sense to give away £67,000 every ten years. Expressed in another way, all other things being equal, it makes sense for older people to make a transfer of capital as soon as they feel comfortable in doing so, in order to start the ten year period running. Provided that they survive ten years, the gift will be 'forgiven' and the individual will have back his £67,000 nil rate band intact.

The problem which applies for most of us is that we cannot afford to give away as much as £67,000. Furthermore, there is the future to be borne in mind, it may be that one's widow/widower will need more capital than can be foreseen, inflation may increase to its former level and so on. Also we may not be sure which members of our families we wish to have our capital, we may be concerned that having too much capital at a relatively early age will spoil their character, tempt them into extravagance, or the wrong sort of company, and so on. Therefore, however much it might make sense *in theory*, from a tax planning point of view, to give away £67,000 every ten years, there will very often be good reasons for not wishing to make outright gifts on this scale.

Trusts

The way round this dilemma is to set up a settlement or 'trust'. This is a way of making a capital transfer while retaining flexibility and control. Expressed in another way, you can retain income from the capital put into the settlement and you can retain the right to ask the trustees to pay the capital back to you. Since you (and where appropriate your wife) can be trustees, you can retain a large measure of effective control.

Insurance companies provide standard 'packages' such as the so-called 'Inheritance trusts' which save a great many of the complications and which enable a person to enjoy the beneficial income tax treatment of investment bonds.

The various schemes offered by insurace companies actually differ from one another in quite important ways, and it is therefore worth analysing the different schemes in some detail.

Inheritance trusts

The original version of this scheme is essentially a means of giving away the future capital appreciation in such a way that it accrues to the person's family and is not part of the person's estate for CTT purposes on his death. This result is achieved in the following way: First, the person sets up a settlement by paying over a relatively small sum such as £1,000. This gift is, of course, covered by the annual £3,000 exemption. The £1,000 is invested in an investment bond issued by an insurance company. The person then makes an interest free loan (repayable on demand) to the trustees of his settlement, and this sum is invested by the trustees either by adding to their investment bond or by their taking out new bonds.

As we have seen earlier, investment bonds are really single premium insurance policies. One attractive feature of the way in which these policies are taxed is that the policy holder may withdraw five per cent of the original investment each year, without any tax liability whatsoever. Under the original type of inheritance trust, the idea is that the trustees will withdraw the five per cent each year and they will use this to repay part of the interest-free loan made to them by the individual who set up the trust. He can then use the sums that he received as repayment of his loan as if they were income, and in many cases the arrangement results in an increase in his 'spendable income'. After twenty years the loan will be completely repaid, leaving all the money in the trust completely free from CTT.

Of course, if the person dies before the twenty years are up, CTT is payable on the portion of the loan not yet paid off, but at least the total tax bill will have been reduced. In a sense, the person's estate will have been 'frozen' and the growth in value of the investment bonds will not form part of the person's estate.

The potential saving of capital transfer tax can be enormous.

Example 14

A puts £100,000 into an inheritance trust and withdraws £5,000 each year for twenty years. At the end of that time the bond will be worth over £208,000 provided average growth of $7\frac{1}{2}$ per cent has been achieved. This will be free from CTT.

Furthermore, the savings are achieved without a serious reduction in the person's flexibility and access to capital in an emergency. At any time, the person can call for repayment of the balance of his loan and this is due to him as of right. Furthermore, the person may also apply to the trustees (of which he may be one himself) for the whole of the trust fund to be paid over to him. If this happens, the CTT benefits will be lost, but nevertheless this flexibility can be very attractive. After all no-one knows how the future will work out, whether you and your wife may need more capital, your other investments may go badly or your attitude towards your children may change. The flexibility built into these plans is therefore very important and setting up an inheritance trust is rather like making a gift whilst reserving the right to ask for your money back.

It must be recognised that, while CTT is being avoided, the trust may come in for a number of smaller tax charges. Higher rate income tax, for example, might arise if the settlor takes withdrawals of more than five per cent a year or on withdrawals made after the full amount of the loan to the trust has been paid off. Broadly speaking, any profit on the partial or total realisation of the trust's investment will be subject to higher rate tax as income of the settlor.

The exact occasion and weight of these taxes cannot be generalised since they depend to a large extent on the settlor's own tax position. What is virtually certain, though, is that they will be considerably lower than any CTT charge had the trust not been established, and these tax liabilities will be an allowable deduction for CTT purposes.

Reverse loan inheritance trusts

One thing that the original inheritance trust did not do was to start the ten year period running. Many people feel sufficiently confident about their financial position and their families to want to make an outright transfer which will escape capital transfer tax completely, provided that they survive ten years. Many insurance companies now offer a more sophisticated type of inheritance trust which seeks to provide exactly this benefit. Once again the trust has the same degree of flexibility so that the person can apply to the trustees for the capital to be paid over to him and from this point of view, there is little to be afraid of in making an outright transfer.

What happens with the reverse loan type of inheritance trust is that the person who set up the inheritance trust takes loans *from* the trustees, instead of loaning them the cash. The person sets up the scheme by making an outright capital transfer to trustees who invest in a bond. Each year, the trustees withdraw five per cent income which is tax free, but instead of using these amounts to repay the loans that the person has made to them, the trustees use the cash to make interest free loans to the person who set up the plan. This type of arrangement has two great advantages:

- The original capital put into the plan escapes CTT after ten years have elapsed.
- The interest free loans made by the trustees to the person who established the plan should count as a deduction for CTT purposes on his death, as they will constitute a debt against his estate incurred for full consideration.

Sometimes people need to use a combination of the two schemes. Since the money put into trust in the reverse loan type of scheme is entirely a gift, it is not normally felt to be prudent to put in more than £67,000 in this way. After all, to the extent to which the capital transfer exceeds the nil rate limit, CTT would actually be payable. Of course, the £67,000 limit applies separately to husband and wife, but if you wish to put in even large amounts, the best way forward is probably to set up a scheme which involves a combination of gifts and interest free loans to the trustees.

Of course, we have had to simplify slightly to get the basic idea across. Care must be taken over the exact tax status of loans made by the trustees. To be fully tax free, the original gift to the trustees must not be regarded by the Revenue as conditional. A recent survey of inheritance trusts advised that, to be safe, all such loans from trusts 'should be at the individual written request of the borrower, and should vary in amount and frequency'. The trustees should also be seen to be exercising their discretionary powers with regard to such loans. There is, moreover, additional administration involved in this method since each annual loan requires a separate written agreement between trustees and settlor for tax records. Nevertheless the reverse loan inheritance trust schemes can be extremely effective and an example of the possible saving is set out below.

Example 15

Mr and Mrs A each put £50,000 into a reverse loan inheritance trust. They take interest free loans of five per cent for twenty years. Assuming that the bond grows by 7½ per cent per annum (before the withdrawals) a total of £308,000 will be taken outside the CTT net (ie the bond will be worth £208,000 and loans of £100,000 will be repayable out of Mr and Mrs A's estates).

PETA schemes

There is a third type of scheme, involving a single premium pure endowment policy and a single premium term assurance policy (thus known as PETA schemes). Though not normally called inheritance trusts, PETA plans aim to do the same thing. These schemes are both more sophisticated and more complicated than the previous two. They are based on the recognition that an investor has two legal rights with regard to his investment: a right to receive the income until he dies and a right to return of capital at his death. PETA plans hinge on the investor keeping the first right but renouncing the second in favour of the trust beneficiaries.

The mechanism is normally as follows: the investor buys a single premium endowment policy with the bulk of the money he wishes to transfer. This provides him with an annual income (the five per cent tax exemption still applies) and does not mature unless the investor is lucky enough to live to 105 years old. At the same time he effects a term assurance policy with a premium of, say, one per cent of the endowment policy premium and settles it in trust for the beneficiaries. As long as the investor dies before 105 the term assurance policy will mature. Under its terms a sum equal to the units in the investment fund allocated under the endowment policy is payable to the beneficiary of the trust.

Because the term assurance policy carries no right of surrender, the Revenue has apparently accepted that the investor has effectively foregone his right to return of capital. It therefore allows a 'discount' for tax purposes on the gift contained in the endowment policy and has agreed a scale of rates with the insurance companies offering the scheme. Thus it is possible, depending on the investor's age and state of health and the amount he wishes to withdraw annually from the endowment policy, for a gift of, say, £100,000 to be valued for tax at less than £67,000. Liability to CTT is thus significantly reduced or avoided altogether.

One advantage of this scheme is that there are no loans to be paid back and the capital is outside the estate immediately. For this reason it is likely to appeal to older investors, though their greater age will reduce the Revenue's discount. To counterbalance this, however, they can opt for a higher rate of annual withdrawal from the endowment policy which will tend to increase the discount.

On the minus side, however, there is little flexibility and they are still looked at with some suspicion by the Inland Revenue. The investor cannot retrieve his capital as easily as he can with the other types of scheme. Nor can he vary the amount he receives annually since this must be fixed at the outset in order to determine his discount. The result is that if the rate of withdrawal exceeds the rate of growth in the value of the units in which his capital is invested then the capital itself will be eroded, perhaps quite considerably.

Caution required

Despite the undoubted usefulness and popularity of inheritance trust schemes they should be approached with some caution. They are not without their critics (many of whom are, admittedly, rivals in the CTT planning market) but there are a number of regular criticisms which should be taken seriously.

First, it is often objected that CTT planning is so individualised — that each case is so different — that no off-the-peg scheme can possibly produce the best results. Certainly, the packages offered by different companies vary widely in flexibility with many offering only one type of trust and only one offering all three main types of scheme. However, the basic inheritance trust schemes probably meet the requirements of most people: it is not that these trusts are defective, rather that they are sometimes used in an inappropriate way.

Before simply signing on the dotted lines provided by a company on its prepared trust documents it is essential for the investor to decide clearly about two things. He must know how much money he wants to transfer as well as the size of income he requires, and also to whom he wants to transfer the money at his death. Without being clear about this he may find he has signed documents setting up the wrong type of trust and the wrong type of scheme.

Another criticism has been that the all-important trust deeds offered in the scheme of some companies were too loosely drafted. The results of faulty trust deeds can have serious repercussions: the settlor may suddenly find himself faced with a tax bill some years into the life of the trust which he had never expected — which, indeed, he had set up the trust to avoid. Alternatively he might find it impossible to change the beneficiaries of the trust as easily as he had expected.

The subject of CTT mitigation is a highly technical one and both of the above criticisms point to a need for good specialist advice. To satisfy the needs of an investor exactly would require the advice of a professional expert in the tax situation and legal technicalities of inheritance trusts. Most companies readily admit this need and many have in-house lawyers who advise on these aspects. However, even these companies frequently recommend that a solicitor, preferably one with experience of CTT, should be appointed as one of the trustees. Not only will this help at the outset but it should also prevent the other trustees doing anything with the funds in the trust later on which might, unknown to them, seriously damage the final tax advantage.

Private discretionary trusts

Accountants and solicitors often recommend people to set up private discretionary settlements as an alternative to insurance arrangements and it is appropriate therefore to describe what is involved.

A discretionary settlement is one where no one beneficiary has an entitlement to income, but the trustees have discretionary powers to pay income (or capital) to any one of a class of beneficiaries. In practice, the class of beneficiaries can be quite small and could include the settlor (ie the person who created the settlement), his wife, their children, grandchildren, etc.

Furthermore, a settlement may be *flexible* in that it may provide for the trustees (at their discretion) to distribute capital to a range of beneficiaries including the settlor. The settlor will not be able to require the trustees to do this as a legal right, but clearly if he is himself one of the trustees he can ensure that his wishes are brought to the attention of the other trustees!

Creating a settlement has legal consequences and should not be contemplated lightly. On the other hand, the settlor and, if appropriate, his wife can be trustees and this will give them a large measure of control over the way in which income is applied, etc. If it is desired that the settlor should himself be a potential beneficiary, it will be necessary to have an outside trustee such as a professional person. In any event, the fact that the settlor may be a trustee will mean that he may retain some control over the way in which the capital is invested and, since many decisions by trustees need to be unanimous, he can effectively retain the power of veto over payments of income or capital to anyone else. Therefore, although a settlor does not have complete control over the capital which is put into a settlement, he does not relinquish control completely.

Income tax

If the settlor is subject only to basic rate tax and not to higher rate tax, there is no disadvantage in his being a potential beneficiary under the settlement.

If the settlor is subject to higher rate tax the position is rather more complex.

There can be income tax benefits from creating a settlement under which the settlor and his wife are excluded from any possible benefit. The income is then treated as the trustees' income and is taxed at forty-five per cent (ie basic rate thirty per cent plus the fifteen per cent 'additional rate' which is charged on such trusts). It may be possible to recover some of the tax charged on the trustees if the income is distributed to beneficiaries who are not subject to tax at a marginal rate of less than forty-five per cent. In passing, it should be noted that the above treatment may still apply even if the settlor's widow may be a potential beneficiary, so long as she cannot benefit during the settlor's lifetime.

In many cases a settlor will wish to be a potential beneficiary under his settlement and may in fact receive most of the income which arises to the trustees. There is clearly no hardship in the settlor being taxed on such income as he actually receives. There is, however, an apparent problem in that any income which arises to the trustees may be assessed on the settlor for higher rate tax purposes, whether or not he actually receives it (unless, as already mentioned, the settlor and his wife are totally excluded from benefit). However, this is a manageable problem as there are ways of minimising taxable income (for example, the trustees might choose to invest in capital growth assets) and, in any event, the settlor is able to recover any tax assessed on him so that he need not actually be out of pocket himself.

Capital gains tax

The trustees are entitled to an annual exemption. This exemption may be limited if the settlor has made other settlements since 7 June 1978, but assuming that there have been no other settlements, the trustees would be entitled to an annual exemption of £2,950. If he has made other settlements the annual exemption is divided between them subject to a minimum of £590 per settlement.

Example of possible saving

B has a portfolio worth £150,000. If he settles shares worth £30,000 he may well save CTT of £18,000 provided that he survives ten years. Furthermore, CTT will not be charged on any capital growth so that if the shares were worth £60,000 after ten years, a further saving of CTT could have been achieved. The capital growth will accrue outside B's estate and will escape CTT on B's death even if B does not survive the ten-year period.

Costs

A firm of solicitors will need to be involved to draw up the trust deed. In practice their fees should normally be within the range of £250–£600. Capital gains tax need not be payable on the transfer of securities to the trustees provided that the trustees are resident in the UK (the hold-over provisions described on p 153 apply to gifts to trustees as well as to gifts to individuals). There will also be administrative expenses, the need for tax returns, and many people prefer the relative simplicity of insurance based schemes.

Making a Will

There are a few actions which give greater benefit for less cost than the making of a Will. Despite this, many people do not have one, and die intestate. The result with even the smallest estate is to cause confusion over who should obtain a grant of representation and administer it. There are also likely to be complications if the estate has to be divided under the intestacy rules. Those with substantial assets may end up paying quite unnecessary CTT and, of course, it may well be that their estate is distributed in a way of which they would not approve.

Intestacy

The law in Scotland is different, but in England and Wales if you die with no children, all your personal possessions will go to your surviving spouse, who will also be entitled to the first £85,000. He or she will have a half share in the remainder of the estate. If your parents are alive they will be entitled to the rest but otherwise the half share will go to any brothers or sisters you may have or to their children.

If you were married and had surviving children, your spouse is still entitled to all the personal possessions, but only gets the first £40,000. He or she gets a life interest in one half of the remaining assets. The remainder goes to your children, who also receive the first half share when your spouse dies. If there is no spouse, but you leave children, the estate is divided equally between them.

When there are neither children nor a surviving marital partner, the estate passes to the parents if they are alive. If they are not, the estate passes to any brothers or sisters, and then on to their children. If this does not produce an heir, the estate will pass to any surviving grandparents, or failing this will go to any aunts or uncles. If this fails to find an heir, the property will pass to the Crown. It is significant that common law wives and husbands obtain no benefit under the intestacy rules.

It is highly improbable that these rules will distribute your possessions in the way that you wish. Even if they do, dying intestate imposes extra burdens on your family which can be easily avoided. It is possible to make a Will yourself, and there are a number of 'do-it-yourself' kits available. On the other hand, the charges that a solicitor will make are comparatively small, so that it normally makes sense to have professional advice.

The formalities

For a Will to be valid under English law, it must be signed in front of two witnesses who must sign the document themselves. Each witness should observe the other's signature as well as that of the testator. On the other hand, the witnesses are only there to affirm that the signature is correct. There is no need for them to know the contents of the Will. A blind person cannot witness a Will, nor can somebody who is mentally ill. Otherwise, anyone can be a witness, although it should normally be someone over eighteen.

If you make your Will yourself, you should be careful to choose witnesses who will not benefit under it. Any gift made to a witness, or the husband or wife of a witness, will be invalid, although this will not affect the rest of the Will. Any amendments or additions to the Will, which may be handwritten, should be initialled by the testator and both witnesses.

Choosing executors

One of the most important points about a Will is choosing the right executors to carry it out. The more complex your affairs, and the more elaborate your Will, the more important this is. Unfortunately, there is no straightforward answer. On the one hand, there are the executor and trustee services offered by the banks and one or two insurance companies. On the other, there is the possibility of appointing a member of the family, and in between the two lies the employment of a solicitor.

If you use a bank, you can be assured that the estate will be administered disinterestedly, and that the technical resources will be available to deal with any complexities which may arise. The bank will, of course, charge for its services; in contrast, a member of the family may well perform the same function for nothing.

The trouble is that Wills frequently lead to considerable ill feeling among families, and this can be greatly accentuated if the executor is himself interested, even if only indirectly. There is also the problem of finding a family member who is properly qualified to carry out the work involved if it is at all complicated.

A solicitor will also make a charge for his or her services but the amount will vary according to the firm chosen. A small firm in the provinces will probably charge less than a large London one. As with a bank, you will have the advantage of impartial administration; if you know the firm well, you can also expect a more personal service.

The most common solution to these problems is to appoint more than one executor. This means that you choose a solicitor, or bank or insurance company and one or two friends or members of the family. The first one can provide the technical knowledge and do the work, while the others can supply a sense of urgency and a personal interest in the case.

Although it is important that Wills should be renewed, they are often left alone for many years. This can mean that when you die, your executors are no longer capable of administering your estate effectively. There is little point in appointing an executor who is the same age or older than you are.

The importance of flexibility

It is often possible to secure considerable tax savings by writing your Will so as to take fullest advantage of the reliefs available to you. The problem is that both the tax law and size of your estate will change. This means that you should regularly review your Will at least once a year so as to make sure that it has not become outmoded. This is clearly impractical and fortunately there is a better and less time-consuming method. This is to leave your executors the discretion to override the dispositions you have made. They can then change the conditions of your Will so as to avoid unnecessary taxation and also to take account of any other changes in conditions which you did not foresee.

This means giving your executors the right to decide how your estate will be distributed. There are, however, a number of safeguards which ensure that this is strictly limited. Usually the Will will be in two parts. The first is quite conventional and disposes of the whole of the estate. It may well give a greater proportion of the assets to the surviving spouse than is likely to be necessary. These provisions will apply unless the executors decide to apply their discretion in the two years after the death. The second part of the Will sets out the executors' powers to override the main section. It sets out those beneficiaries to whom they can decide to distribute part of the estate. If a husband is concerned that too much may be given to other beneficiaries, he can make his widow one of the executors with a power of veto on any distributions. The same can of course be done by a wife who is concerned about her husband.

It is difficult to know how to divide your assets unless you know when you are going to die. If a man leaves a widow in her early sixties, he will probably want to leave her a considerable sum. She will need a house, and a sufficient income to maintain her independence. At the same time, she will want some reserves to guard her against inflation or other economic reverses over the next twenty or thirty years. There is no point in doing this for a widow in her eighties who is already in poor health.

In this case, there is every advantage in passing as many assets as possible over to a younger generation once the widow's needs have been taken care of. At the very least, it will make sense to take advantage of the £67,000 nil rate band. When assets are passed over, the beneficiaries may request that these should be given to their own children. This will give rise to income which is taxable only at the rate appropriate to them, rather than being aggregated with that of the parent.

A particular advantage of this arrangement is that the executors can have up to two years to decide whether or not to exercise their powers. Any action they take is backdated to the date of death, and taxation is assessed on that basis. This can be valuable since it means that the executors are able to act on the basis of knowledge which the testator could not possibly have possessed, enabling the Will to take account of both economic changes and altered circumstances within the family. Of course, CTT is due to be paid at the normal times, so that if the exercise of the executors' discretion creates a liability which is settled late, interest must be paid. This could well be the case when the whole of the estate has been left to the widow and it is decided to reduce the future CTT bill which would have to be paid when she died, by using some of the lower rates of tax on the husband's estate.

If this type of Will is contemplated it is essential that it is drawn up by a solicitor.

The alternative

If a Will has not been written on a discretionary basis, a similar effect as a last resort can be achieved if those who benefit under it either disclaim or vary its provisions. It is usually only possible for a disclaimer to be effective when the successive interests in the property are free from doubt, either because of the way they are set out in the Will or because of the intestacy rules.

A disclaimer or variation made within two years will enable a person to transfer assets with no personal CTT or CGT implications. Hence, it permits post-death tax planning to be made by the beneficiaries, even if the deceased did not provide for it. On the other hand, it is normally more cumbersome and less efficient for income tax purposes than arranging the matter through a discretionary Will.

Summary

If you do not make a Will, your assets will be disposed of according to the intestacy rules. Even if this broadly meets your intentions, the process is tiresome. There is, therefore, every reason to make a Will.

One of the most important points is the choice of the right executor or executors. There is much to be said for combining one or more members of the family with a disinterested person or organisation if the estate is complex. When it comes to writing a Will, there are strong arguments in favour of making it discretionary since there may be a long period between the writing of the Will and the time when it takes effect. If the Will is not discretionary, and turns out to be inefficient for tax purposes, much can be done by post-death deeds of disclaimer or variation.

Once you have made your Will, lodge it with your lawyer or bank and file a copy with your personal papers, together with a note saying where the original has been placed. It is also worth appending a schedule to both copies giving details of your bank accounts, solicitors, accountant, stock broker, life insurance policies, building society accounts, savings certificates, shares, property owned at home and abroad and any other information that will enable your executors to handle matters promptly for the beneficiaries. Don't hide away the odd million in a numbered Swiss bank account without giving anybody the details. It has happened!

16 Retirement abroad

It is necessary to begin by setting out the rules which govern residence status as it does not necessarily follow that you will cease to be resident in the UK for tax purposes even though you acquire a home abroad. This is crucially important. If an individual continues to be regarded as UK resident he will generally remain subject to UK tax on his worldwide income. On the other hand, if he is not resident for tax purposes his liability will be confined to UK source income such as rents, dividends and interest from UK companies and pensions paid by a former UK employer. Furthermore, a non-resident who is also not ordinarily resident will not normally be subject to CGT.

Residence

The Inland Revenue practice has evolved in a piecemeal way and is largely based upon decided cases. There is relatively little legislation which bears directly on the matter and what little is said raises almost as many questions as it answers. For example, the Taxes Acts clearly contemplate that an individual can be resident in the UK even though he is absent from the country for the entire year! However, certain aspects of Revenue practice are clearly defined.

Available accommodation

If you have accommodation available for use in the UK, you are resident here for any year in which you as much as set foot in this country. This is the position even if you do not actually use the accommodation. Moreover, the accommodation may be regarded as available even though you do not own it.

A decided case showed that the availability of a shooting lodge in Scotland was sufficient to make a foreigner resident for years when he came to the UK, and the retention of a suite of rooms at a hotel or a club could also render you 'resident' if they were kept in a 'permanent state of readiness' for your use.

There is an exception to this general rule if you are working full time abroad — the exemption does not continue after you have retired.

This does not necessarily mean that you will have to sell your property in the UK; you could let it, for instance, although a tax liability would arise on the rents that you received. Or it may be that you can escape by claiming under a double tax treaty. Several of these treaties contain provisions whereby people resident both in the UK and another country may be treated as resident of only one country. But these are exceptions to the general rule that in order to achieve non-resident status you must not have available accommodation.

Visits to the UK

You will be regarded as resident if you spend 183 days or more in any year in this country. The Revenue booklet contains the ominous statement: 'There are no exceptions to this rule', (although in practice a dually resident individual may still be able to establish that he should be treated under the provisions of a double tax treaty as if he were not resident). The Revenue normally ignores the day of arrival and departure, but there have been cases where fractions of days have been taken into account, so it would be wise to err on the side of caution.

Even if the 183 days test does not apply, you may still be treated as resident if you make regular visits to the UK which average more than three months per annum, measured over a four year period.

Example 16

A has been resident abroad for a number of years, but begins to make visits to the UK. The periods spent in the UK each year are as follows:

1982/83	51 days
1983/84	98 days
1984/85	170 days

If he spends 45 days or more in the UK during 1985/86 his visits will have averaged 91 days per annum and he will be regarded as having become resident again from 6 April 1985. If he does not visit the UK at all during 1985/86 he will be able to spend 95 days in the UK during 1986/87, as he will then be just within the limit for the period 1983/84 to 1986/87.

These rules permit some room for manoeuvre in that a continuous period may span two different tax years. It could be, for example, that A spent a single period of 268 days in the UK from 29 December 1983 until 22 September 1984 and still escaped being treated as resident because 98 days fell in the 1983/84 tax year and 170 in 1984/85.

Husband and wife treated separately

Rather surprisingly, since husband and wife are looked at together for most tax purposes, they are taken separately for residence purposes. It is quite conceivable therefore that A could be non-resident but have a resident wife, although if she has accommodation in the UK this will be regarded as available for his use. If A were non-resident his wife would normally be regarded as a separated person for tax purposes, and income tax and CGT would be charged only on her income and gains.

Ordinary residence

The CGT legislation imposes a liability on individuals who are resident or ordinarily resident for a year of assessment. Ordinary residence corresponds to *habitual* residence so that an individual may remain ordinarily resident for an isolated year when he happens not to be resident. However, this should not be a problem for a person who is retiring abroad as the Inland Revenue will treat a person as not resident or ordinarily resident if he leaves the UK for a period of at least three years.

Claims under double tax treaties

It is possible for an individual to be resident in several countries. A number of double tax treaties contain provisions whereby a dually resident person may be treated as if he were a resident of only one country, and set out rules for determining the position. Typically, the tests will be:

(a) If the individual has a permanent home in only one country that is where he will be deemed to be resident.

(b) If the position has not been resolved by (a) then the individual is to be treated as resident where he has the centre of his personal and economic interests.

(c) If the above tests do not resolve the position, the individual is treated as resident where he has an habitual abode.

(d) If he has an habitual abode in both countries, he is deemed to be a resident of the country of which he is a national.

It will be obvious that these tests can be rather uncertain and if you can so arrange matters, you should seek to resolve the position by having no home in the UK. The centre of your personal and economic interest may be in the UK if your family reside here and most of your income and assets are in the UK. Nevertheless, the provisions of certain double tax treaties may be a useful safety net if you find that you have inadvertently made yourself resident in the UK for a particular year. Unfortunately, not all countries have double tax treaties with the UK and some treaties do not contain these provisions. Countries with relevant clauses in their double tax treaties include France, Italy, Portugal, Spain, Switzerland and the United States.

Procedure

Strictly speaking, you are resident or non-resident for a year of assessment. However, in practice the Revenue treats individuals as not resident and not ordinarily resident for part of a year of assessment. The Revenue summarises its procedure in Booklet IR 20 as follows:

> If a person claims that he has ceased to be resident and ordinarily resident in the UK, and can produce some evidence for this (for example, that he has sold his house here and set up a permanent home abroad) his claim is usually admitted provisionally with effect from the day following his departure. Normally this provisional ruling is confirmed after he has remained abroad for a period which includes a complete tax year and during which any visits to this country have not amounted to an annual average of three months.

> If, however, he cannot produce sufficient evidence, a decision on his claim will be postponed for three years and will then be made by reference to what actually happened in that period. During the three intervening years, his tax liability is computed provisionally on the basis that he remains resident in the UK. He therefore continues to receive the various income tax reliefs due to a resident

of the UK except for any tax year in which he does not set foot in the UK. His liability is adjusted, if necessary, when the final decision is made at the end of three years.

Domicile

In the longer term, your domicile may be more important than your residence status. As we have seen, capital transfer tax is charged on lifetime capital transfers and on death. CTT applies to *all* property worldwide if the transferor is domiciled in the UK (whether or not he is resident here), whereas it applies only to transfers of UK assets if the transferor is domiciled abroad. Similarly, there are income and CGT implications since a foreign domiciled individual who is resident in the UK is not chargeable on overseas income and gains unless they are remitted to this country.

Domicile is a different concept from residence. As we have seen, you can be resident in more than one country but you can only have one domicile. You are domiciled where you regard yourself as 'belonging' or (put another way) where you intend eventually to make your permanent home. Nationality and residence are relevant factors, but are not conclusive in themselves, and it is quite conceivable that a person may reside in a country for a number of years for personal and/or financial reasons and yet still not be domiciled there. There is a difficult onus of proof which needs to be satisfied before the Revenue and the courts will be satisfied that an original domicile has been abandoned and a new 'domicile of choice' has been acquired.

In practical terms, it will be hard for a person of UK origin who is retiring abroad to establish that he has become domiciled there. If a UK property is retained the Inland Revenue will naturally conclude that the individual had not finally resolved to live the rest of his life abroad, and that he remains legally domiciled in the UK.

Similarly, if that individual eventually returns to the UK the Inland Revenue will argue that he was domiciled in this country for the whole of his life, notwithstanding that he spends a long period abroad.

If mitigation of CTT is a serious consideration, then it will be advisable to establish a foreign domicile as soon as possible as CTT is levied on an individual's worldwide estate if he dies within three years of having had UK domicile. The Revenue's domicile questionnaire is included overleaf. Steps to be taken which may help to establish foreign domicile, according to the *Allied Dunbar Tax Guide*, are:

(1) Develop a long period of residence in the new country.

(2) Purchase or lease a home.

(3) Marry a native of that country.

(4) Develop business interests there.

(5) Make arrangements to be buried there.

(6) Draw up your will according to the law of the country.

(7) Exercise political rights in your new country of domicile.

(8) Arrange to be naturalised (not vital).

(9) Have your children educated in the new country.

(10) Resign from all clubs and associations in your former country of domicile and join clubs, etc. in your new country.

(11) Any religious affiliations that you have with your old domicile should be terminated and new ones established in your new domicile.

(12) Arrange for your family to be with you in your new country.

The above are some of the factors to be considered and the more of these circumstances that can be shown to prevail, the sooner you will be accepted as having changed your domicile.

INLAND REVENUE DOMICILE QUESTIONNAIRE

Name: .... Reference: ....

The following information is requested in order that the claim to be not domiciled in the United Kingdom may be given consideration.

1   Where and when were you born?   _____

2   In what country was your father domiciled at the date of your birth? (In the case of a country with a Federal system, the particular State, Province, etc should be stated.)   _____

3   What changes, if any, took place in your father's domicile during your minority?   _____

4 If your father is dead, state his full name and the date and place of his death.

5 In what country do you consider that you are domiciled and on what grounds? (In the case of a country with a Federal system, the particular State, Province, etc should be stated.)

6 Whether any accommodation is retained for your use in that territory and, if so, the address, the nature of the accommodation and whether it is kept in a permanent state of readiness for your occupation.

7 What are your business, personal, social or other connections with that territory?

8 If you are married, where do your spouse and any children reside?

9 Is any accommodation retained for your use in the United Kingdom and, if so, the address and nature of the accommodation?

10 What periods have you spent in the United Kingdom during each of the past 10 years?

11 The reason for your residence in the United Kingdom, eg whether in connection with business or employment (in which event, details of the business or employment and the nature of the position held should be stated), or the education of children.

12 What are your intentions for the future; and if not to stay permanently in the United Kingdom, the circumstances in which it is envisaged that residence will cease?

Date: .... Signature: ....
Address: ....
....
....

Tax Planning in Year of Departure

The most important considerations are usually the timing of retirement, departure abroad and the avoidance of CGT problems on the sale of assets such as a business or shares in a family company.

Golden handshakes

Because of the rules which govern top-slicing relief (see p 94) it will be beneficial in many cases for a person to terminate his employment at the very beginning of a tax year during which he retires abroad. The relief will be maximised if you retire on 6 April and then immediately cease to be resident.

Commutation of pension rights

In principle it must make sense if you retire abroad to commute your pension entitlement for a lump sum. If you do not do so, you will have more pension income arising in this country which will be subject to UK tax. If you take a capital sum in commutation you may well be able to invest it in a way whereby it attracts tax neither in the UK nor in the country where you reside.

Capital gains tax

Sale of main residence

The crucial thing to bear in mind when considering CGT is that it is the date that contracts are exchanged which fixes the date of disposal — not completion date. So it will not avoid CGT if you exchange contracts whilst you are still resident even though you may cease to be resident before you receive payment.

In many cases, it is simply not practical to defer the exchange of contracts until you have left the United Kingdom. It may be possible to give your solicitor a power of attorney to act in your absence—but this may also produce practical problems.

Fortunately it will often not matter anyway — no chargeable gain generally arises on the disposal of a main residence, but it is necessary to outline the exceptions to that general rule in case they apply in your particular situation. The flow chart opposite should make the position clear.

Sale of main residence

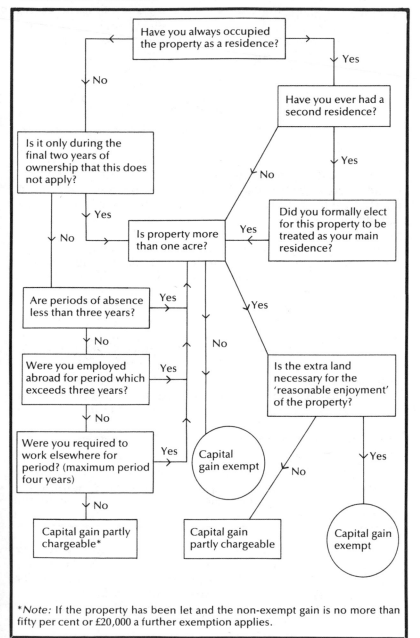

Note: If the property has been let and the non-exempt gain is no more than fifty per cent or £20,000 a further exemption applies.

Sale of Business

It is more difficult to avoid CGT on the sale of a business. By the very nature of things, a purchaser will wish there to be continuity of trading and will not just be acquiring assets which are used in a trade. Indeed, there will often be a significant element of goodwill in the price, and this definitely requires continuity. The problem is that a vendor will not be able to avoid CGT by deferring a sale until he has ceased to be UK resident as CGTA 1979, s 12 makes these types of gains subject to CGT if the non-resident has traded in the UK through a branch or agency.

This is a complex area where it would be sensible to take professional advice. The Inland Revenue practice is unclear, but it may be that no liability will arise if you cease to be resident part way through a tax year and dispose of the business before the next 5 April. Certainly letters from Technical Division have suggested this interpretation but Inland Revenue practice and interpretation do change from time to time and more recent articles in the professional press suggest that Somerset House is reconsidering its position.

There are sometimes ways of avoiding this problem. For example, a relief is given if a trader disposes of a business and re-invests in new business assets within three years ('roll-over-relief'). Somerset House has confirmed that this relief may be available even though the trader emigrates and re-invests in an overseas business. It is, however, necessary that the whole of the sale proceeds are re-invested to obtain full relief.

Example 17

B sells the goodwill of his business for £100,000 and realises a capital gain of £65,000. If he re-invests £100,000 in appropriate business assets the whole gain may be rolled-over, but if he only re-invests £75,000 then £25,000 capital gain will remain chargeable.

In some cases, of course, the position may be covered by retirement relief. A more risky idea if all else fails, and here you will definitely need to take professional advice, is to transfer your business to a limited company in return for shares (this need not give rise to a CGT charge) and to sell the shares after you have shaken off UK residence. When you seek professional advice explain that the transfer to a limited company must come within the provisions of CGTA 1979, s 123. This is an uncertain solution because of the recent trend by the courts to 'look through' transactions entered into only for fiscal or tax avoidance purposes. You should also ask about professional fees. It is one thing to take a calculated risk on a tax avoidance scheme, without compounding the problem by incurring substantial accountancy and legal costs!

Sale of a company

Much the same problem arises if you wish to sell a private company and cannot conveniently delay the sale until you become non-resident. The commercial logic of the situation may require your presence in the UK to negotiate and conclude the sale contract, and provide managerial assistance during a 'hand-over' period.

The position has been easier to deal with where an intending emigrant has been trading through a limited company rather than as a sole trader or partnership, as a well-tried technique has been available whereby a sale could be effected for commercial purposes without it constituting a disposal for CGT purposes. One uses the past tense because the recent policy adopted by the courts (especially in the House of Lords case of *Furniss* v *Dawson*) has strongly suggested that the Inland Revenue may be able to undermine such arrangements and render them ineffective. The following suggestions have to be read in the light of these comments.

'Put' and 'Call' option arrangements

The classic technique has consisted of the vendor and intending purchaser entering into reciprocal option arrangements whereby the vendor had the legal right to 'put' the shares, or require the other party to purchase them, and the other party acquired an option to 'call' for the shares, or require the vendor to sell them to him. There are no cases which have come before the courts where the Inland Revenue has successfully attacked this device, but it is thought that the Inland Revenue might well succeed in such an attack, following the *Furniss* case.

An alternative arrangement that is more likely to succeed is for a vendor to take Loan Stock rather than cash, and for the Loan

Stock to be redeemed after the individual has established non-resident status. No capital gain normally arises on a disposal of a controlling interest in a private company in return for securities issued by the acquiring company, but it is strictly necessary for advance clearance to be obtained under the provisions of CGTA, s 88 and you should ensure that your accountant puts his mind to formulating a clearance application at an early juncture. To some extent the commercial disadvantages of having loan stock rather than cash can be mitigated by the loan stock being secured against particular assets of the company being sold or those of the acquiring company.

Tax treatment when abroad

As mentioned, liability for income tax on UK income continues even though the recipient is not resident in the UK. Directors' fees from UK companies and pensions are subject to UK tax. Withholding tax is deducted at source at the rate of thirty per cent from dividends and interest. These can sometimes be avoided if there is a double tax treaty in force.

Directors' fees and pensions

Directors' fees and remuneration from UK companies will normally remain subject to income tax. Certain double tax treaties provide a possible exemption which covers other types of earned income, for example the relevant part of the UK–USA treaty states:

(*Article 14 Independent personal services*)
Income derived by an individual who is a resident of the United States from the performance of personal services in an independent capacity may be taxed in the *USA*. Such income may also be taxed in the UK if, *and only if*:
(a) the individual is present in the United Kingdom for a period or periods exceeding in the aggregate 183 days in the tax year concerned, or
(b) the individual has a fixed base regularly available to him in the United Kingdom for the purpose of performing his activities, but only so much thereof as is attributable to services performed in the United Kingdom.

(*Article 15 Dependent personal services*)
Remuneration derived by a resident of the United States in respect of employment exercised in the US shall be taxable only in the USA if:

(a) the recipient is present in the United Kingdom for a period not exceeding in the aggregate 183 days in the tax year concerned, and

(b) the remuneration is paid by or on behalf of an employer who is not a resident of the United Kingdom, and

(c) the remuneration is not borne as such by a permanent establishment or a fixed base which the employer has in the United Kingdom.

The UK–USA Treaty is chosen because it has served as a model as other treaties have been re-negotiated.

Pensions are also normally subject to UK tax, but here again double tax treaties may provide exemption. The UK–USA Treaty stipulates that pensions paid to a resident of the USA shall be taxable only in the USA unless the pension is paid by the UK government or local authority when it may be taxed in the UK. However, UK tax is not charged if the pensioner is a US national as well as resident in the USA.

Dividends

A non-resident is not normally entitled to the 'tax credit' (ie, tax deducted at source). But, if your investment income is sufficiently large there may be a liability for higher rate tax.

Example 18

C receives UK dividends of £21,000. If he were resident in the UK he would be entitled to tax credits of 3/7ths, ie £9,000 (these credits can be reclaimed to the extent that the individual is entitled to allowances). However, a non-resident is not normally entitled to claim them (but see p 184 on claims under ICTA 1970, s 27) and C may have a higher rate tax liability computed as follows:

Taxable income	*£21,000*

Higher rate tax due:

First £16,200	Nil
£3,000 @ 10%	300
£1,800 @ 15%	270
Total tax payable	£570

The situation may well be different if the individual can claim under a double tax treaty as many of these provide that the recipient can reclaim part of the tax credit and is not subject to higher rate tax. The relief under the treaties generally operates in the following way:

Example 19

C would be entitled to claim the tax credits and to reclaim half so that the effective rate of UK withholding tax is fifteen per cent, ie:

UK dividends	£21,000
Tax credits	9,000
	30,000
Withholding tax 15%	4,500
Repayment:	
Tax credits	9,000
Less: withholding tax	4,500
	£4,500

Interest

Untaxed interest is theoretically liable to UK tax but the Inland Revenue does not generally pursue such tax. Extra-statutory Concession B13 states:

> Where a person not resident in the United Kingdom receives interest (eg bank interest) without deduction of income tax and is not chargeable in the name of agent under the Taxes Management Act 1970, s 78 no action is taken to pursue his liability to income tax except so far as it can be recovered by set-off in a claim to relief (eg for proportionate reliefs and allowances under the Income and Corporation Taxes Act 1970, s 27) in respect of taxed income from United Kingdom sources.

An agent for these purposes is a person who can instruct the bank etc on payments and transfers from the account.

From 1985/86, UK residents will normally receive interest net of tax at the composite rate, but this system will not apply to individuals who are not ordinarily resident and they will be able to receive interest gross by signing a certificate confirming to the bank etc that the beneficial owner of the deposit is not ordinarily resident in the UK.

A number of double tax treaties exempt foreigners from UK tax on interest income or specify that UK tax shall not exceed a specified rate.

Countries with relevant treaties include: Italy, France, Malta, Portugal, Spain, Switzerland and the United States.

Exempt gilts

Interest paid on certain British government securities is exempt from income tax provided that the beneficial owner is neither resident nor ordinarily resident in the United Kingdom. The relevant securities are listed below. It should be noted that the exemption applies only if the non-resident holds the stock at the date that the interest is paid and does not apply where the non-resident has sold the stock even though the sale may have been 'ex-div'. The Inland Revenue is understood to apply a strict interpretation to the exemption and have denied repayment in such cases.

Application for repayment and, for payment of interest, without deduction should be made on Forms A1 and A3 obtainable from: Inspector of Foreign Dividends, Lynwood Road, Thames Ditton, Surrey KT7 0DP.

Gilts exempt from tax for non-UK residents:

$3\frac{1}{2}$%	War loan 1952 or after	9%	Treasury 1994
$5\frac{1}{2}$%	Treasury 2008–12	9%	Treasury 1992–96
$5\frac{3}{4}$%	Funding 1987–91	$9\frac{1}{2}$%	Treasury 1999
6%	Funding 1993	$12\frac{1}{2}$%	Treasury 1993
$6\frac{1}{2}$%	Funding 1985–87	$12\frac{3}{4}$%	Treasury 1992
$6\frac{3}{4}$%	Treasury 1995–98	$12\frac{3}{4}$%	Treasury 1995
$7\frac{3}{4}$%	Treasury 1985–88	13%	Treasury 1990
$7\frac{3}{4}$%	Treasury 2012–15	$13\frac{1}{4}$%	Exchequer 1996
8%	Treasury 2002–6	$13\frac{1}{4}$%	Treasury 1997
$8\frac{1}{4}$%	Treasury 1987–90	$13\frac{3}{4}$%	Treasury 1993
$8\frac{1}{2}$%	Treasury 1984–86	$14\frac{1}{2}$%	Treasury 1994
$8\frac{3}{4}$%	Treasury 1997	$15\frac{1}{4}$%	Treasury 1996
9%	Conversion 2000	$15\frac{1}{2}$%	Treasury 1998

Rental income

Anybody who rents UK property is required to deduct basic rate tax (thirty per cent) from any rents paid to a non-resident landlord. This obligation exists even if the rent is paid into a UK bank account. Moreover, the obligation to deduct basic rate tax applies to the gross amount of the rent, so that if the landlord incurs expenses he is obliged to make a repayment claim. The only way of avoiding these deductions is for the rent to be collected by a UK agent. Rent paid to an agent is paid without any tax deduction as the agent becomes liable for assessment. However, the assessment is on the net amount after deducting allowance expenses, so this provides a valuable cash flow benefit.

The following expenses are normally allowable:

- Agents Fees;
- Interest on mortgages and similar loans (the £30,000 limit does not apply); subject to the property being let for six months of the year, and being available for letting all year;
- An allowance of 10 per cent of the net rents for wear and tear to furniture.

Offshore investment companies

If no relief is due under a double tax treaty, and the investment income is sufficiently large to make the individual subject to higher rate tax, it may make sense to transfer the securities to an offshore investment company. There will then be no UK liability beyond the tax withheld at source. It will generally be sensible to carry out such transfers after you have left the UK as there may otherwise be CGT problems.

Personal allowances

You are generally entitled to personal allowances only if you are resident here, although non-resident British subjects may make a claim for a proportion of the allowances to which they would be entitled if they were resident (a claim under ICTA 1970, s 27). The way in which this relief is computed is to calculate the income tax liability which would arise if you were UK resident and the whole of your income were subject to the UK tax. The resultant figure is then subjected to the fraction

$\dfrac{\text{UK Income}}{\text{World income}}$ and if the product is less than the tax withheld at source from UK income, the individual is entitled to a repayment.

Example 20

D has UK income of £15,000 and foreign income of £5,000. He is a bachelor and even if he were resident in the UK he would be entitled only to a personal allowance of £2,205.

Relief under s 27 would be computed as follows:

Total income	£20,000	(including foreign income)
Less: personal allowance	2,205	
	£17,795	
Tax on £17,795 =	£5,498	

$\dfrac{\text{UK income}}{\text{World income}} = \dfrac{15}{20}$ and $\dfrac{15}{20} \times £5,498 = £4,123.00$

UK tax on £15,000	£4,500.00
Relief under s 27 =	£ 376.50

Foreign taxes

The above has set out the UK tax position, but if you are retiring abroad you will need to explore carefully the tax system in the country in which you will reside. It is likely that the basic rules for computing assessable income will be quite different from those which apply in the UK and you will obviously need to take competent local advice.

General strategy: finding out more

Tax legislation changes with bewildering frequency, both in the United Kingdon and abroad . Once you have decided to retire abroad you should make enquiries via the embassy concerned about current rates of tax and allowances. The international firms of accountants (Touche Ross, Deloittes, Price Waterhouse, etc) publish information guides on doing business in most developed countries. However, these guides, usually free of charge, are not up-dated every year so you will still need to check with local accountants and advisors. Beware of the mental trap of assuming that the foreign tax system incorporates the same exemptions as our own. For example, we have an exemption from CGT for gilts which have been held for more than twelve months, but you may well find that if you settle in (say) Florida that a CGT liability could arise under United States tax legislation. Remember that the base cost for foreign CGT purposes may remain your original cost and not the market value when you take up residence abroad. Certain countries such as Canada do compute gains in this way but they are the exception rather than the rule.

Another anomaly worth mentioning also arises in connection with gilts. It is the practice on sales of short gilts (less than five years to redemption) for the seller to receive an adjustment which represents the interest which has accrued on a daily basis. This is not at present subject to income tax in the United Kingdom (although possible changes are on the way), but if you are resident in the United States for example, it does constitute taxable income.

Other financial considerations

The position on United Kingdom retirement pensions needs to be carefully explored. After all you have paid in for these benefits for most of your working life! If you have already reached sixty-five before you retire abroad, there is no problem. You should notify the DHSS so that suitable arrangements can be made. You will, however, have your pension frozen unless you reside in an EEC country or one of those countries which has a reciprocal arrangement with the UK in which case you will continue to qualify for annual increases. The DHSS issue two helpful booklets, SA29 'Your Social Security and Pension Rights in the European Community' and N138 'Social Security Abroad'.

Even if you have not yet reached the statutory retirement age you will still generally qualify for a National Insurance retirement pension in due course, but the amount may be restricted unless you have a full 'contribution record'. There is generally no obligation to pay contributions if you are resident abroad, but it may pay you to make class 3 voluntary contributions if you are nearing retirement. These will safeguard your right to a full pension. And, provided you reside in an EEC country, they could be a sensible investment in that the benefits will be 'index linked' and the prospective return is, therefore, very attractive.

Foreign exchange controls

These vary immensely, but the current position in the UK is relaxed compared to other countries. There is unlikely to be any problem at the present time if you reside in another EEC country, but even here the position may change according to the political climate. You may well not foresee any likelihood of wishing to return to the UK or moving to another country, but why not keep the position as flexible as possible? Preserve your options as far as possible. Find out when you will become subject to exchange controls (this does not usually happen until you have been resident in a country for several years) and investigate what action you could take (for example making a settlement) which could lessen your exposure.

Inheritance law

Again bear in mind that foreign legal systems are quite different from our own. For example the inheritance laws in Guernsey require a fixed proportion of a deceased person's estate to pass to his children. This kind of rule applies in many continental countries and needs to be borne in mind. Is it what you want to happen? If not, then you need to take legal advice on ways in which you may be able to circumvent these rules, perhaps by making a separate English will, or creating a settlement.

Purchase of a property overseas

Property like any investment has its share of pitfalls. Do remember that the legal situation in any country can change overnight. There are, however, some general rules which apply wherever you are thinking of buying. They may sound obvious, but British people have a tendency to do rash things when in an unfamiliar environment. The combination of sunstroke and the local wine can leave the unwary signing things that they would not dream of signing back home.

First and foremost, do *not* try to dispense with the services of a lawyer. On the contrary, sensible people engage one in Britain (usually their own solicitor), and another in the area chosen for their retirement.

Do use a reputable agent, preferably one affiliated to a professional surveying body, or FOPDAC (Federation of Overseas Property Developers, Agents and Consultants, 55 Sidney Street, Cambridge). You might also consult the useful guide to buying property abroad which is produced by Euro Property Advisors, 27A New Street, Salisbury.

Do not part with any money, however much you are impressed by the developer or the agent, other than through a bank or lawyer. Then at least you will have tangible evidence to support your claim to have purchased the property.

Never buy off a plan, unless a large section of the development is already completed. If you must do so, however, insist on a bank or insurance company guarantee of completion. Check the development's water and electricity sources.

The choice of property is so wide and the pressure of the sales pitch so enticing that you must be firmly prepared before you negotiate. Prepare a checklist and make the agent or vendor complete a copy. You should get a majority of ticks and the negatives will help you to reduce the price if it has been pitched artificially high. Even the price of a new property is subject to negotiation, no matter what the brochure says.

You will want to know the details that will have a direct bearing on the lifestyle you wish to enjoy. Particularly if you are looking at an apartment.

(1) Is the development predominantly English occupied or multi-national?
(2) Can I meet one or two of the occupants?
(3) Is membership of any of the following clubs included: beach, riding, golf, country, tennis, bowls?
(4) If not, where are the nearest centres for these sports and are there any special concessions on membership fees?
(5) Is there a heated swimming pool?
(6) Is a garage included?
(7) Is there a club room and bar?

(8) Is there a clinic with an English speaking doctor in the complex?
(9) Is there a telephone included or a telephone point?
(10) Is there a bus service to the nearest town?
(11) Is there a taxi point and what is the fare to the nearest town/airport?
(12) What security arrangements exist? 24 hour patrol? Telephone linked to a central point?
(13) Is there a television point?
(14) Does it include a mooring?
(15) Is a safe or any furniture included in the price?
(16) Can somebody build in front of the beautiful view?
(17) Will the developer maintain an office on the site?
(18) What are the charges for the upkeep of communal gardens, swimming pool and outside painting, etc? How often are they revised?
(19) Where is the nearest shopping complex and does it contain a pharmacy?
(20) Is the apartment air-conditioned?
(21) Does it include the following: dishwasher, washing machine, refrigerator, waste disposal unit and bathroom heater?

It will be impossible to get twenty-one ticks but some developments offer most of these benefits and you should be able to score fourteen or above. Your own priorities will determine whether these fourteen will be sufficient to warrant a purchase.

17 Retiring to the UK—a tax haven!

It is a little known fact that the UK is a tax haven for persons of foreign domicile who settle here. If you are not domiciled in the UK and have overseas income and capital gains, you need not pay tax unless you remit them here, so payment of UK tax on overseas income and gains becomes a *voluntary* activity, provided that you can arrange your affairs in the right way!
We have already discussed the concept of domicile and it will be apparent that you may reside in the UK for a number of years and still not be domiciled here. A special rule applies for capital transfer tax purposes whereby you will be deemed to be domiciled in the UK if you have been resident for seventeen of the preceding twenty tax years, but this rule does not affect the favourable treatment for income tax and capital gains tax purposes.

The most important steps to take from a practical point of view are the establishment of several different offshore bank accounts so that capital and accumulated income can be clearly identified. The point is that if you make remittances to the UK from a 'mixed' account which contains both capital and accumulated income, the Inland Revenue will argue that the remittances are to be identified primarily with income: ie the worst possible basis! However, this potential problem is easily overcome by opening separate offshore bank accounts.

Basically, the balance on your account at the date you come to the UK to take up residence is regarded as capital. In future, overseas income should be credited to a separate account, and this includes interest on your existing overseas bank account. Furthermore, a third account needs to be opened to receive the proceeds of sales of overseas securities and other foreign assets which show capital gains. Other sale proceeds should be credited to your main capital account.

Obviously, your strategy should be to live off your capital account, and to supplement this (if necessary) by remittances from the account which contains capital gains. Only as a last resort should you make remittances from the income account. In this way you will legitimately have minimal overseas income and gains to declare.

Furthermore, there are a number of ways in which you can use the balance on your overseas income account without incurring a UK tax liability. Firstly, you can spend the money outside the UK (for example on holidays) or you can invest it (but be careful of the way in which you deal with the position when you sell the investment or you may end up remitting income without meaning to do so). In an emergency you may be able to rely on court decisions which indicated that a husband who gives his wife accumulated overseas income is not liable to income tax when she remits it, as it is capital in her hands! However, you should take professional advice before doing this in view of the recent trend of House of Lords' decisions (the *Furniss* case again).

Another point that is worth bearing in mind, but needs careful handling, is if you have just one overseas investment and you sell it. It is arguable that accumulated income from this particular source may be safely remitted in the following tax year. It would be sensible to discuss this with your accountant or professional adviser first, but this is another possible way of remitting money to the UK without incurring an income tax liability.

A foreign domiciled person is still liable to tax in the normal way on income and gains arising in the UK, so you should avoid UK investments. If you wish to invest in the UK Stock Market the best way is to do so via an offshore fund in the Isle of Man or Channel Islands and many unit trust and investment groups have funds which meet this requirement.

An individual can realise chargeable capital gains of £5,900 per annum without any CGT liability, so if you have no UK capital gains it may be wise to remit an appropriate part of the capital gains account. This will then avoid a tax liability if you should need to draw heavily on this account in a later year.

Capital transfer tax planning

Until the seventeen year rule bites, you will not be subject to CTT on capital transfers of foreign assets. Foreign assets include money held in overseas bank accounts, shares in foreign companies and bearer securities actually held overseas. It may well be wise to hold UK property through a foreign investment company as the shares in such a company are 'excluded property' (ie, not subject to CTT when owned by a person of foreign domicile), and this effectively converts UK assets into foreign property.

As the seventeen year deadline approaches, it may also be appropriate to make a settlement of overseas assets as this will take them outside the ambit of CTT even though you may subsequently be deemed to have UK domicile. Substantial savings of CTT are possible by taking steps of this nature, but it is essential to take competent professional advice.

Expatriates returning to the UK

Expatriates who return to the UK do not generally qualify for any income tax or CGT concessions. They become liable to UK tax on their worldwide income and gains once they become resident and ordinarily resident in the UK. Tax planning in these situations consists mainly in timing the date of return, and ensuring that certain pitfalls are avoided.

Checklist for expatriates about to return to the UK

- Should capital gains be realised before you resume residence in the UK and become subject to CGT? Will there be a sale of a UK property and, if so, will it be covered by the main residence exemption?
- Should capital gains be realised before the start of the tax year in which you return to the UK (this will normally be advisable if you have been non-resident for less than thirty-six years)
- Should UK bank deposit accounts be closed before the date of return to avoid UK tax liability interest? However, consider possible liability for foreign tax.
- Consider ways of 'bringing forward' income on foreign securities etc, eg by selling stocks cum-div and repur-

chasing ex-div. Should foreign bank deposit accounts be closed immediately before you return to the UK? Again you should bear in mind the possible tax implications in the foreign country in which you are resident.

● Ensure that salary for any terminal leave period will not attract UK tax—normally it will be covered by the 100% deduction.

● There may be cases where liability for VAT can be avoided by arranging for professional advisors to invoice you while you are a non-resident.

Golden handshakes

Finally, it is worth mentioning in this context that a special relief may be available for expatriates who return to the UK and receive a golden handshake after their return (see p 175).

A termination payment is completely exempt where foreign service represents seventy-five per cent of the total period of employment or (where the employment lasted more than twenty years) at least fifty per cent of the period was spent in foreign service during the last twenty years. The definition of foreign service is that the employee was either not resident or not ordinarily resident or entitled to the 100 per cent deduction as having met the 365 day test.

Example 21

A was non-resident in the UK from 1966 to 1976. He then qualified for the 100 per cent deduction from 1976 until 1980, so that he was not subject to UK tax on his salary even though he was resident. In December 1984 he retired and received compensation of £80,000 *14 years* = 77% and so the compensation of 18 years £80,000 is exempt.

Where the above conditions are not satisfied the employee is entitled to an extension to the £25,000 exemption available to UK residents generally which is determined by the formula:

$$\frac{\text{Foreign service}}{\text{Total period of employment}}$$

This fraction is applied to the amount of the golden handshake after deduction of the £25,000 exemption.

Example 22

Suppose A's employment had started in 1970. The fraction

$$\frac{\text{Foreign service}}{\text{Total period of employment}}$$

then becomes 71%, so the compensation is not completely exempt. The taxable amount would be arrived at as follows:

Compensation	80,000
Less: 'normal exemption'	25,000
	55,000
10/14ths thereof	39,286
Taxable amount	£15,714

Example 23

If A had other taxable income of £28,000 (including his salary from the job) the tax payable on the £15,714 would be computed as follows:

Total taxable income	£43,714	tax thereon	£19,188.40
Deduct tax payable on income	£28,000		£10,395.00
			£ 8,793.40

Tax actually payable on the £80,000 compensation is
50% of £8,793.40, ie £ 4,396.70

Index